THE USBORNE
ENCYCLOPEDIA
OF
PLANET
EARTH

SCHOLASTIC INC.

New York   Toronto   London   Auckland   Sydney
Mexico City   New Delhi   Hong Kong

THE USBORNE
ENCYCLOPEDIA
OF
PLANET
EARTH

Anna Claybourne, Gillian Doherty and Rebecca Treays

Designed by Laura Fearn and Melissa Alaverdy

Consultant: Dr. William Chambers

Managing designer: Stephen Wright

Managing editors: Felicity Brooks and Jane Chisholm

Cover design: Stephen Wright, Laura Fearn and Zöe Wray

Digital images: John Russell and Nicola Butler

Picture research: Ruth King

Page 1: aerial view of the Grand Prismatic Spring,
Yellowstone National Park, U.S.A.
Pages 2-3: the Chicago skyline, U.S.A.
This page: computer-enhanced image of an iceberg

CONTENTS

Some words in this book have an asterisk* after them. This means that you can find out more about them on the page listed in the footnote.

The Earth and its moon

PLANET EARTH

THE EARTH IN SPACE

The Earth may seem enormous, but it's actually just a tiny speck in a universe made up of billions of stars and planets. Its position in relation to the Sun is very important. The Sun provides the heat and light which we need to survive.

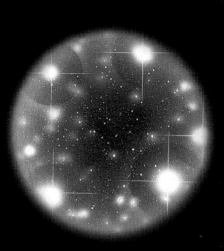

The universe is everything; not just the billions of stars and planets, but the vast spaces in between.

This picture shows the nine planets in our solar system in the correct order, although they are not to scale.

The Sun

Mercury

Venus

Earth

Mars

Jupiter

Saturn

Neptune

Uranus

Pluto

Our solar system

Stars are huge balls of hot gas which give off heat and light. Most stars look tiny, but that's just because they are far away. The nearest star to Earth is the Sun.

A planet is an object that travels around, or orbits, a particular star. As each planet moves, it also spins around on its own axis (an imaginary line running through the planet). The Earth is one of nine planets that orbit the Sun. Together they make up our solar system.

The Earth spins around on its axis as it orbits the Sun.

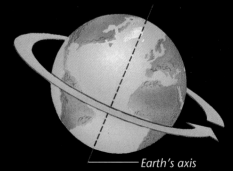

Earth's axis

The Moon

Most of the planets in our solar system have moons. A moon orbits a planet in the same way that a planet orbits a star. Earth has just one moon, but some planets, such as Saturn, have several. It takes almost 28 days for the Moon to orbit the Earth.

As the Moon orbits the Earth, it rotates. It takes exactly the same amount of time to spin around once as it does to travel around the Earth. This means that when we look at the Moon from the Earth, we always see the same side of it.

This picture of the Moon was taken from the Apollo 11 satellite*.

Living Earth

Earth is the third planet from the Sun. It is the only known planet with the right conditions to support living things, although scientists are searching for life on other planets.

The Earth's distance from the Sun means that it receives just the right amount of heat and light. Its combination of gases enables plants, animals and people to breathe, and it is warm enough for water to exist as a liquid. All of these things are essential for life on Earth.

Galaxies

Our solar system is part of a galaxy called the Milky Way. A galaxy is a cluster of millions of stars. Galaxies are so big that it can take a ray of light thousands of years to travel across one. There are 6,000 million known galaxies in the universe, but there could be many, many more.

The Milky Way galaxy

LOOKING AT THE EARTH

We now have a more accurate picture of the world than ever before. Modern technology has meant that scientists can monitor vast areas of the Earth from space. Even inaccessible places, such as deserts, ocean floors and mountain ranges, have been mapped in detail.

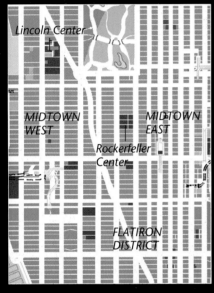

A map showing the layout of streets in Manhattan, New York, U.S.A.

Maps of the Earth

A map is a diagram which gives information about a particular area. Maps can show anything from road layouts to the shape of the land. Some focus on small areas, but others show the whole of the Earth's surface. The size of a map in relation to the area it represents is called its scale. If a map's scale is 1:100, it shows an area 100 times its size.

Flattening the Earth's surface

Because the Earth is roughly spherical, the best way to represent it accurately is as a globe. In order to produce flat maps of the Earth's surface, cartographers (map-makers) have to stretch some areas and squash others. Different kinds of maps give the countries slightly different shapes and sizes. These different views of the Earth's surface are called projections*.

The most accurate flat map of the world looks like pieces of orange peel.

Dividing lines

On maps, imaginary lines are used to divide up the Earth. These help us to measure distances and find where places are. The lines that run horizontally are called lines of latitude and the lines that run vertically are known as lines of longitude. The distance between the lines is measured in degrees (°).

Some of the lines used to divide up the Earth have special names. The most important ones are shown on this globe.

Arctic Circle

Tropic of Cancer

The Equator

Tropic of Capricorn

*Projections, 147

Satellite observation

Artificial satellites are man-made devices which orbit the Earth, moons, or other planets. They observe the Earth using a technique called remote sensing. This means that instruments on the satellite monitor the Earth without touching it. Some satellites orbit the Earth at a height of between 5km (3 miles) and 1500km (930 miles), providing views of different parts of the Earth. Others stay above the same place all the time, moving at the same speed as the Earth to give a constant view of a particular area. These are called geostationary satellites. They travel at a height of around 36,000km (22,370 miles).

Sensing

Satellites use a range of remote sensing techniques. One useful type is radar. It can provide images of the Earth even when it is dark or cloudy. Radar works by reflecting radio waves off a target object. The time it takes for a wave to bounce back indicates how far away the object is.

Cameras are used to photograph the Earth's surface. The images are converted into electrical pulses and beamed to Earth. Some cameras use a form of radiation known as infrared. Different types of surfaces reflect infrared light differently, so it's possible to obtain images of the Earth which show the varieties of land surfaces. This can be useful for monitoring vegetation.

Prime Meridian line

This ERS-1 satellite is used to collect information to help scientists study climate change.

Satellite uses

Information provided by satellites enables experts to produce accurate maps, predict hazards such as volcanic eruptions or earthquakes, and record changes in land use around the world. Sensors can also reveal day-to-day changes, such as whether soil is wet or dry, and there are even satellites especially for monitoring weather.

This satellite image of the Earth shows its different types of land surfaces.

THE SEASONS

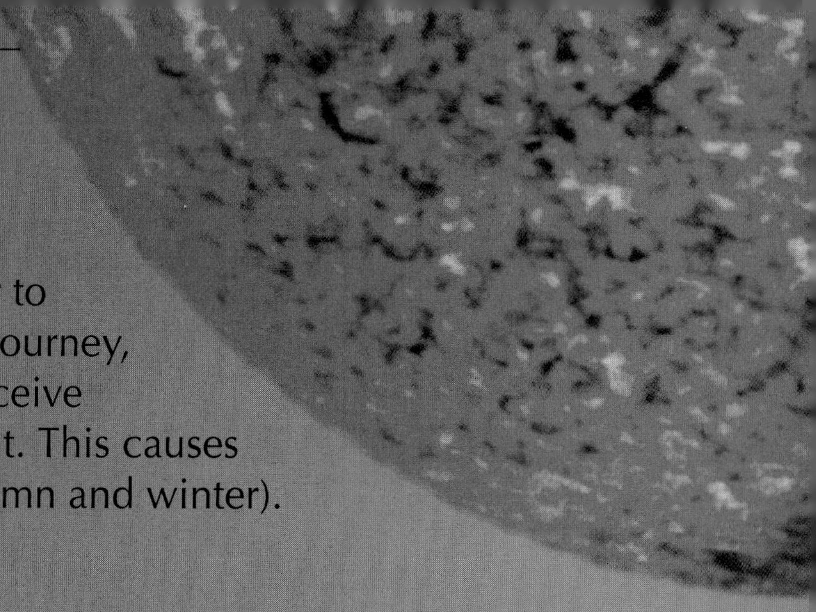

The Earth takes just over a year to orbit the Sun. As it makes its journey, different parts of the world receive different amounts of heat and light. This causes the seasons (spring, summer, autumn and winter).

Tilting Earth

The Earth is tilted at an angle as it travels around the Sun. This means that one hemisphere is usually closer to the Sun than the other. The hemisphere that is nearer the Sun receives more heat and light energy than the one that is tilted away. So in this half it is summer, while in the other it is winter.

As the Earth orbits the Sun, the half that was nearer the Sun gradually moves further away, so that eventually it becomes winter in this hemisphere and summer in the other. In June the Sun's rays are most concentrated at the Tropic of Cancer and in December they are most concentrated at the Tropic of Capricorn.

In June, it is summer in the Arctic. The summer only lasts for six to eight weeks.

Most of the year, it is winter in the Arctic because it is tilted away from the Sun.

The diagram below shows how the seasons change as the Earth orbits the Sun.

March: Neither hemisphere is tilted more towards the Sun.

Spring

Autumn — — Equator

Summer

Winter

Sun's rays

Winter

Summer

Autumn

Spring

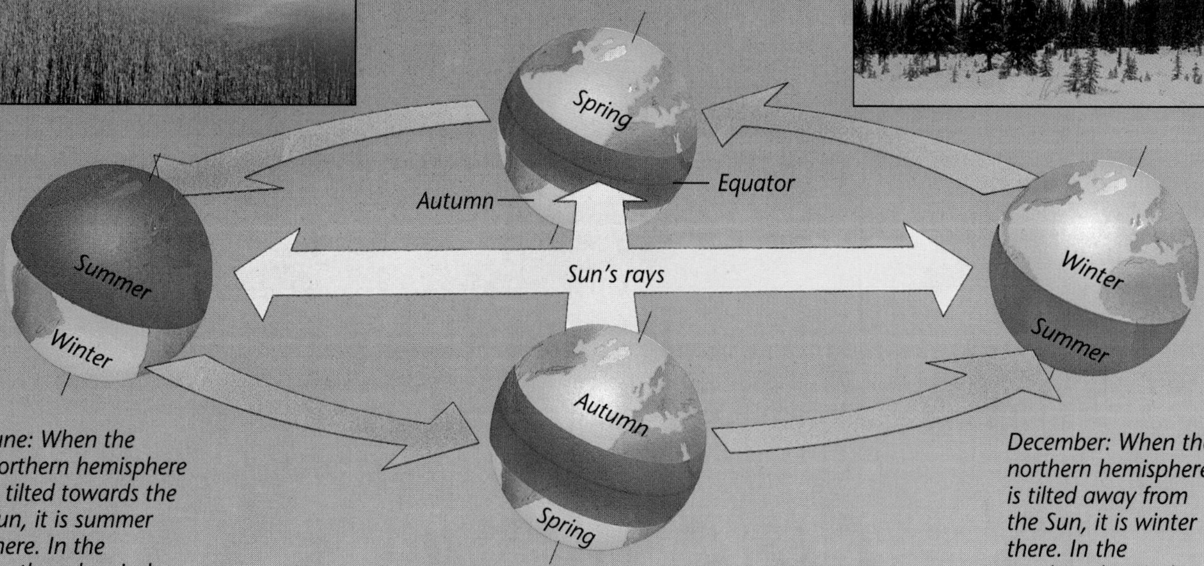

June: When the northern hemisphere is tilted towards the Sun, it is summer there. In the southern hemisphere, it is winter.

September: As in March, neither hemisphere is tilted more towards the Sun.

December: When the northern hemisphere is tilted away from the Sun, it is winter there. In the southern hemisphere it is summer.

The heat and light that the Sun gives out are essential for life on Earth.

Leap years

The time it takes for the Earth to orbit the Sun is called a solar year. A solar year is 365.26 days, but as it is more convenient to measure our calendar year in whole days, we round the number down to 365. In order to make up the difference, every four years we have to add an extra day to our calendar year, making it 366 days. These years are called leap years*. The additional day is February 29th. However, this does not make up the difference exactly, so very occasionally the extra day is not added.

Equatorial seasons

The Earth is hottest where the Sun's rays hit its surface full on. But because the Earth's surface is curved, in most places rays hit the ground at an angle. This causes them to spread out over a larger area, which makes their effect less intense.

However, at areas near the Equator, rays hit the Earth almost at a right angle throughout the year. This means that the temperatures there are high all year round. Temperatures are also affected by the distance the Sun's rays have to travel through the Earth's atmosphere. This distance is less for areas near the Equator than it is at the poles, which means that less heat energy is absorbed by the atmosphere.

This picture shows how the Sun's rays spread out as they reach the Earth's surface.

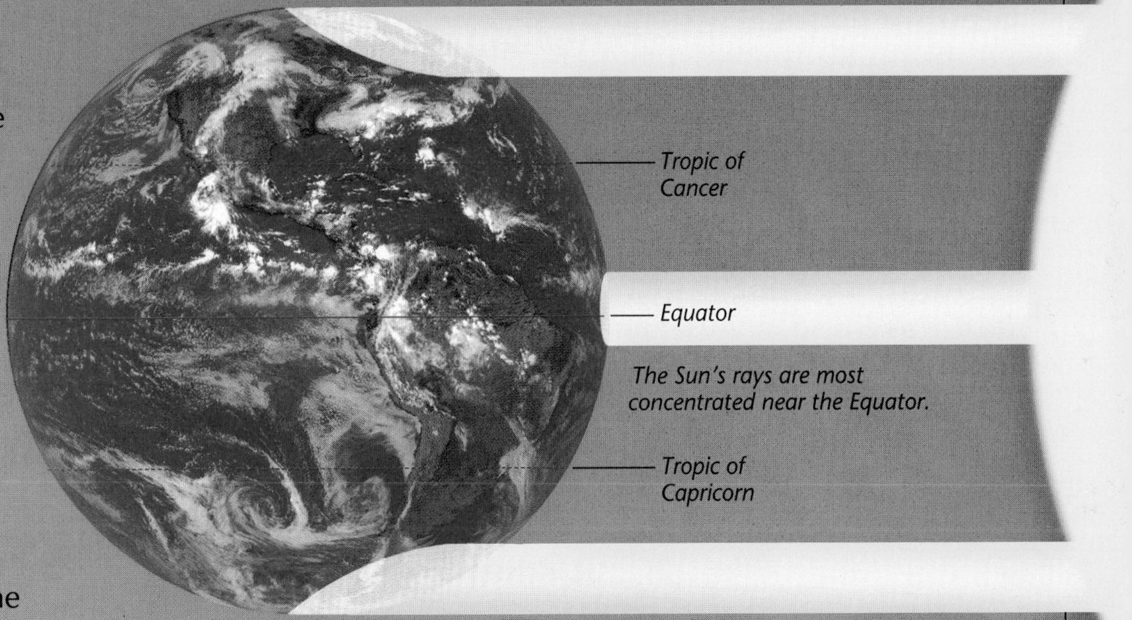

Tropic of Cancer

Equator

The Sun's rays are most concentrated near the Equator.

Tropic of Capricorn

The Sun's rays spread out at the poles and have further to travel through the Earth's atmosphere.

Near the poles, the midday Sun is low on the horizon, making temperatures cool.

Near the Equator, the midday Sun is high in the sky and its rays are very intense.

*Leap years, 148

DAY AND NIGHT

When it's daytime in Australia, it's night-time in South America. This is because the Earth spins around on its axis as it orbits the Sun, so the part of the Earth that faces the Sun is constantly changing.

Day and night

It takes 24 hours, or one day, for the Earth to spin around once. As it rotates, a different part of the world turns to face the Sun. The part of the Earth that is turned towards the Sun is in the light (daytime), but as it turns away from the Sun it becomes dark (night-time).

This diagram follows the change from day to night in one place (marked by the flag) as the Earth spins.

Path of orbit around the Sun

Sunrise and sunset

In the morning, you see the Sun "rise" in the sky. This is only an illusion. In fact, the Sun doesn't move at all, but as your part of the Earth turns to face it, the movement of the Earth makes it seem as though the Sun is rising. When your part of the Earth turns away from the Sun at night, it looks as if the Sun is sinking in the sky until eventually it disappears over the horizon. This is called a sunset.

In the morning, the Sun looks as though it's rising, as your part of the Earth gradually turns to face it.

In the evening, the Sun seems to sink down in the sky, as your part of the Earth turns away from it.

Daylight hours

Everywhere in the world, apart from places that are on the Equator, days are longer in the summer than in the winter. This is because the hemisphere where it is summer receives more sunlight than the hemisphere where it is winter.

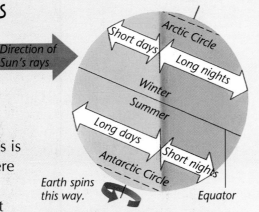

Direction of Sun's rays

Short days

Arctic Circle

Long nights

Winter

Summer

Long days

Short nights

Antarctic Circle

Earth spins this way.

Equator

This diagram shows how the length of day and night varies depending on the time of year and where you are on the Earth.

Midnight Sun

The area north of the Arctic Circle is known as the Land of the Midnight Sun, because during the summer it is daylight there all the time. Because the northern hemisphere tilts towards the Sun in summer, the Arctic Circle doesn't turn away from the Sun, even at night. In winter, by contrast, it is dark there all the time because the northern hemisphere tilts away from the Sun. The same thing happens in the southern hemisphere, in the areas south of the Antarctic Circle.

This shows the Sun in the Arctic Circle in the middle of the night. During the summer, the Sun is visible there all the time.

Moon shapes

The Moon doesn't give out any light of its own. It looks bright to us because we see the Sun's rays reflected off its surface. During the day, we can't usually see the Moon because the Sun is brighter.

As the Moon orbits the Sun and we see different amounts of its sunlit side, its shape seems to change as shown in these diagrams.

Direction of sunlight

Moon

The pictures below show what the Moon looks like from Earth when it is in each of the positions numbered above.

1. New moon
2. Crescent
3. Half moon
4. Waxing
5. Full moon
6. Waning
7. Half moon
8. Crescent

INSIDE THE EARTH

The Earth is not solid. It has a solid surface, but inside it is made up of different layers, some of which are molten, or liquid. If you sliced through the Earth, you would see three main layers: a hard outer shell called the crust, the mantle and the core.

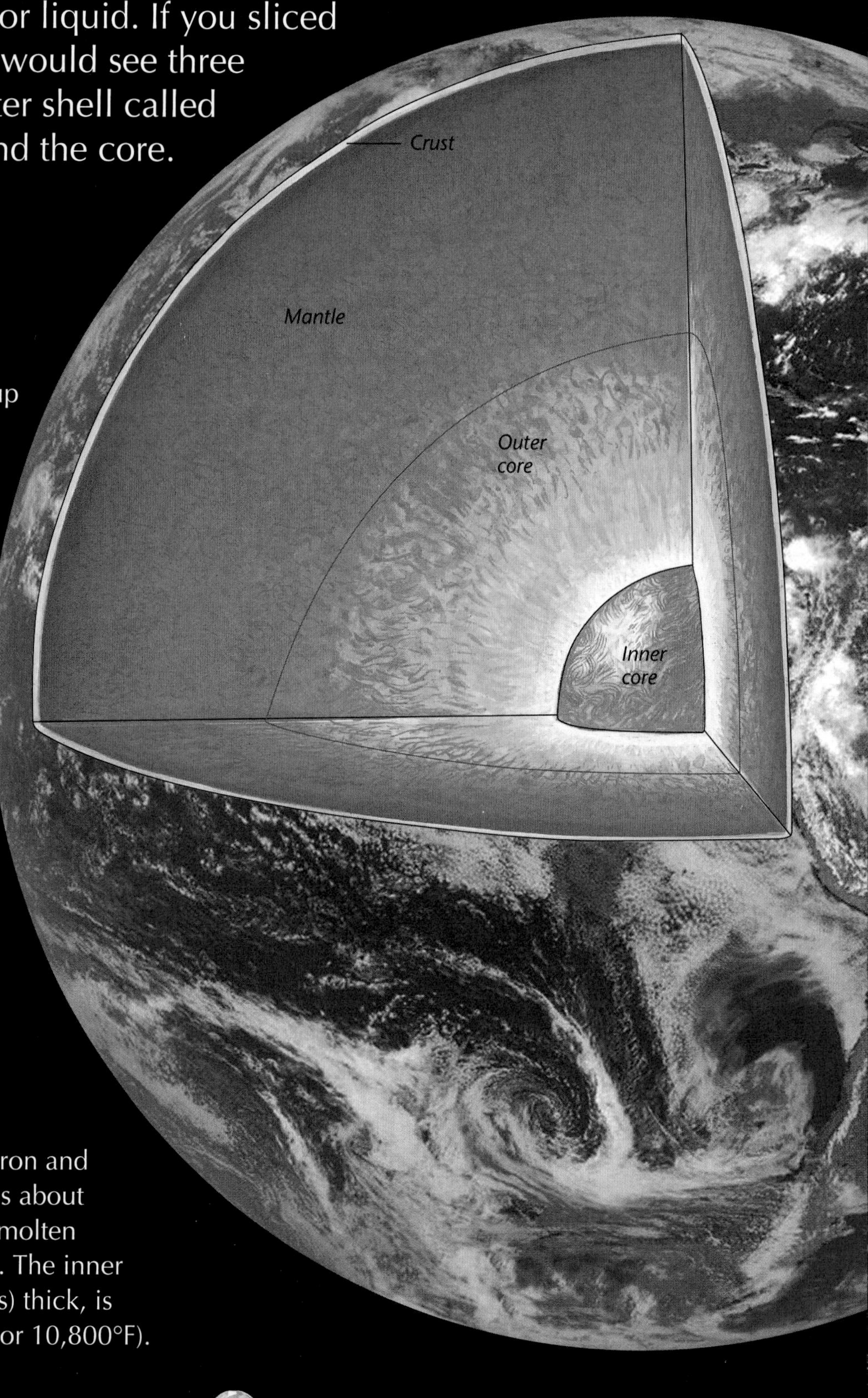

The structure of the Earth

The picture on the right shows the different layers that make up the Earth, though the layers are not drawn to scale.

The thinnest layer is the crust. It is between 5km (3 miles) and 70km (43 miles) thick. Below this is the mantle which is made of silicon and magnesium. The mantle is about 3000km (1900 miles) thick.

The upper and lower parts of the mantle are solid rock, but the middle layer is so hot that the rock has melted to form a thick substance called magma. The solid upper layer and the crust float on this liquid layer.

The core is probably made of iron and nickel. The outer core, which is about 2200km (1400 miles) thick, is molten whereas the inner core is solid. The inner core, about 1300km (800 miles) thick, is extremely hot (about 6,000°C, or 10,800°F).

Crust

Mantle

Outer core

Inner core

The Earth's crust

There are two different types of crust. Thick continental crust forms land, and much thinner oceanic crust makes up the ocean floors. Continental crust is made of granite, which is a light rock. Oceanic crust is made of a heavier rock called basalt.

The Earth's crust is made up of oceanic and continental crust.

Oceanic crust is 5-10km (3-6 miles) thick.

Continental crust is 20-70km (12-43 miles) thick.

Ocean

Investigating the Earth

It's difficult to find out about the inside of the Earth. Geologists, who study rocks, find out about areas near the surface by drilling holes into the crust and collecting rock samples. But they can only drill a short distance below the surface.

Volcanic eruptions provide some information about material deep inside the Earth. But the main way that geologists find out about the Earth's structure is by studying earthquakes. During an earthquake, vibrations called seismic waves travel through the Earth. As they pass through different materials, they change speed and direction. By studying records of earthquakes, called seismograms, geologists try to work out what rocks are at different depths.

Earthquake

Paths of waves

This diagram shows how seismic waves change direction as they pass through the Earth.

Magnetic Earth

The Earth is magnetic. This may be caused by molten iron in its core. It is as if the Earth has a huge magnetic bar in the middle. The ends of this "magnet" are called the magnetic poles. These are not in exactly the same place as the geographic North and South poles.

This diagram shows the Earth's magnetic field: the area affected by its force. The lines show the direction of the magnetic field.

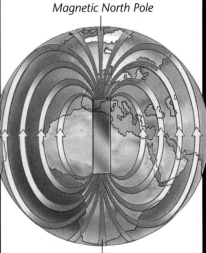

Magnetic North Pole

Magnetic South Pole

You can see this magnetic force at work when you use a compass. The compass needle, which is magnetic, always points north. This is because it is pulled, or attracted, by the magnetic North Pole.

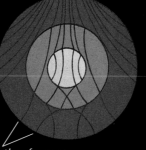

A compass's magnetic needle always points north.

THE EARTH'S CRUST

The Earth's crust is broken up into large pieces which fit together like a giant jigsaw puzzle. The pieces are called plates. Many of the Earth's most spectacular features have been formed, over many thousands of years, by the movement of these plates.

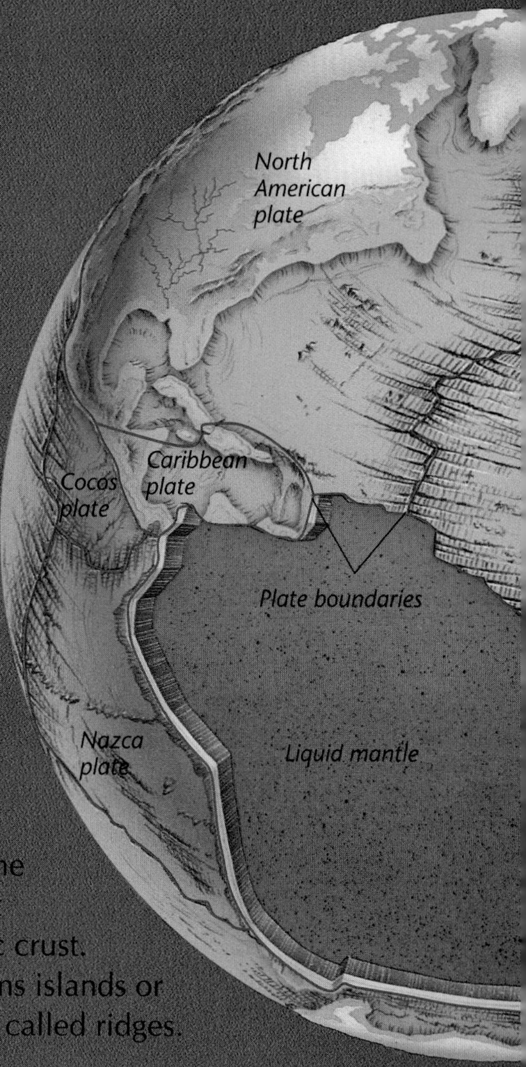

North American plate

Cocos plate

Caribbean plate

Plate boundaries

Nazca plate

Liquid mantle

A moving surface

The Earth's crust is divided into seven large plates and several smaller plates. Each one is made up of either continental or oceanic crust, or both. The edges of the plates, where they meet, are called plate boundaries.

The plates float on the liquid mantle and are constantly moving. Their movement is usually slow, an average of 5cm (2in) a year, which is roughly the rate at which your fingernails grow. They can move toward one another, spread apart or shift sideways. Because all the plates fit together, movement of one plate affects all the others.

Ocean features

When plates on the ocean floor move apart, magma from the mantle rises and fills the gap. Boundaries where this happens are called constructive boundaries. As the magma reaches the surface, it hardens to make new oceanic crust. The new crust sometimes forms islands or underwater mountain ranges, called ridges.

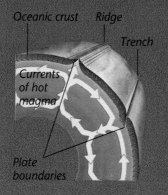

Oceanic crust *Ridge*

Trench

Currents of hot magma

Plate boundaries

When plates push together, underwater trenches form as one plate is forced below another. These boundaries are called destructive boundaries. The deepest trench, the Marianas Trench in the Pacific Ocean, is deeper than Mount Everest is tall.

This diagram shows how ridges and trenches form.

Shifting continents

As plates shift, the position of the oceans and continents on the Earth's surface changes. The maps on the right show how geologists think the continents may have shifted.

Geologists think that there was once a single supercontinent, which we call "Pangaea".

As new rock formed at plate boundaries, the floor of the Atlantic Ocean probably widened.

Today, South America and Africa are drifting apart at a rate of 3.5cm (1.5in) each year.

Atlantic Ocean

Africa

South America

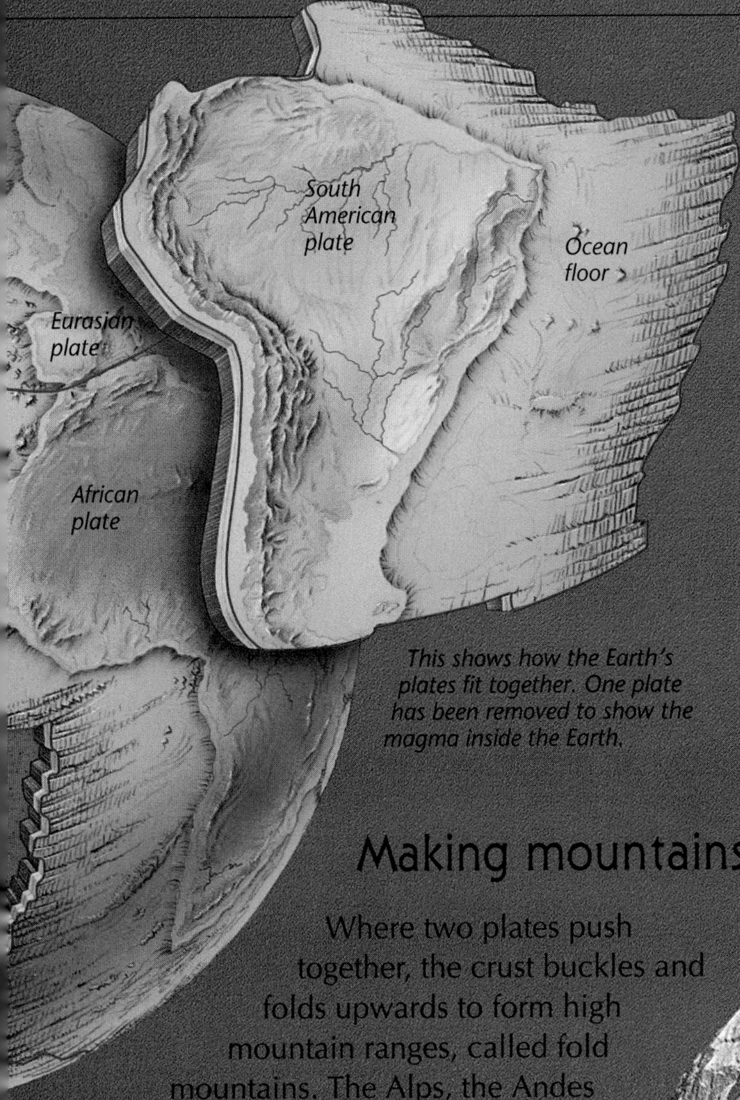

South
American
plate

Ocean
floor >

Eurasian
plate

African
plate

*This shows how the Earth's
plates fit together. One plate
has been removed to show the
magma inside the Earth.*

Faults

As plates move, the strain of the movement sometime causes brittle rock at plate boundaries to crack. These cracks are called faults. When two faults are close together, the chunk of crust between them can sometimes collapse, to form rift valleys. The raised parts on either side form mountains called block mountains.

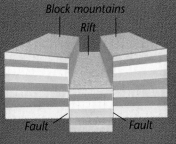

Block mountains
Rift
Fault   Fault

This picture shows a fault in the Great Rift Valley in Africa.

Making mountains

Where two plates push together, the crust buckles and folds upwards to form high mountain ranges, called fold mountains. The Alps, the Andes and the Himalayas are all fold mountains. The Earth's crust is thickest where fold mountains form.

*This is part of the
Himalayas mountain
range in Asia,
which is the
highest in the
world.*

ROCKS, MINERALS & FOSSILS

T he Earth's crust is made up of rock. There are three kinds of rocks: igneous, sedimentary and metamorphic. Over many years, rocks are sometimes transformed from one kind to another.

Igneous rock

Igneous rock gets its name from the Latin word for "fire", because it is formed from hot molten rock from inside the Earth. When this molten rock, or magma, cools, it forms solid igneous rock. The way that the magma cools determines the kind of igneous rock that is formed.

Tuff is an igneous rock made from pieces of volcanic rock and crystals compressed together.

Obsidian is a shiny igneous rock formed when magma cools quickly.

Sedimentary rock

Sedimentary rock is made from tiny pieces of rocks and the decayed remains of plants and animals. These fragments, called sediment, are usually blown by winds, or carried by rivers or landslides, to the sea, where they sink. The water and upper layers of sediment press down on the lower layers, until eventually they form solid rock.

Chalk is a sedimentary rock made from tiny sea creatures.

Sandstone is a sedimentary rock made up of sand grains.

The Grand Canyon, U.S.A., is a gorge formed by the Colorado River. You can see the layers of sandstone. Layers of rock like this are called strata.

Metamorphic rock

Metamorphic rock is rock that has been changed by heat or pressure. It can be formed from igneous, sedimentary or other metamorphic rocks. Its name comes from a Greek word meaning "transformation". The texture, appearance and chemical composition of the rock can be altered by heat from magma or pressure caused by plate movements.

Marble is a metamorphic rock formed from limestone.

Mica schist is a layered metamorphic rock.

Minerals

Rocks are made from substances called minerals, which in turn are made up of simple chemical substances called elements. If you look at a rock with a magnifying glass, you can sometimes see the different minerals it contains. Some minerals are cut and polished to be used as gemstones.

These pictures show minerals in rocks and as gemstones.

Opal can be milky white, green, red, blue, black or brown.

Turquoise runs through rock in the form of veins.

Carnelian is a dark red stone.

Fossils

The shapes or remains of plants and animals that died long ago are sometimes preserved in rocks. They are called fossils.

Fossils are formed when a dead plant or animal is buried by sediment which turns to sedimentary rock. Usually the remains decay, although hard parts such as teeth, shells and bones can sometimes survive. The space left by the plant or animal fills up with minerals which preserve its shape.

The fossil of an ammonite (an extinct sea creature)

THE EARTH'S RESOURCES

Iron is extracted from its ore in a blast furnace.

The Earth provides all sorts of useful rocks, minerals and other materials. We quarry stone and sand for building and glassmaking, extract over 60 types of metal, and mine hundreds of useful chemicals and compounds such as salt, talcum and silicon.

Metals

Metals are among the most important materials we get from the Earth. They are strong, yet they can be beaten out into flat sheets or drawn out to make wire. They also conduct electricity and heat well. They have a range of properties: some, such as iron, are very strong;

some, including calcium and lithium, have medical uses; and precious metals, such as silver and gold, are used to make necklaces, bracelets and other decorative items.

Most metals are found in ores, types of rocks that contain a metal in the form of a chemical compound. Metals are extracted from ores by mixing them with other chemicals to cause a reaction.

Iron ore, coke (a type of coal) and limestone go in here.

The furnace is over 30m (100ft) tall.

Iron ore, coke and limestone react with each other in a blast furnace to make new chemicals, leaving the iron free.

Molten iron flows out here.

Hot air is blasted into the furnace.

Waste called slag comes out here.

People have used precious metals for centuries as attractive settings for precious stones like these.

More minerals

As well as metals and stone, the Earth provides many other chemicals and elements which have thousands of uses, often depending on how hard they are (see the scale of hardness opposite). For example, corundum is used to make sandpaper and silicon is used in electronic circuits.

The Mohs scale

The hardness or softness of minerals is measured on a scale of 1 to 10, called the Mohs scale. Soft minerals, such as talc, crumble easily into powder. On the other end of the scale are the hardest minerals, such as diamonds, which are used in cutting tools.

Talc 1

Gypsum 2

Calcite 3

Fluorite 4

Each number on the Mohs scale is accompanied by an example mineral.

Apatite 5

Orthoclase 6

Quartz 7

Topaz 8

Corundum 9

Diamond 10

Silicon chips

Silicon comes from a rock called quartz. It has become very important in modern society, because it is used to make the electronic chips that run computers, digital watches, mobile phones and millions of other everyday appliances.

A silicon chip

Building materials

Rocks and minerals from the Earth are used to make bricks, cement, glass and other building materials. Stone for building is usually extracted from the ground in quarries. It's often so hard and heavy that explosives have to be used to blast it apart first.

Sand is made of rocks, minerals and sometimes seashells, ground down to fragments by the action of water (which is why it is usually found near the sea). Concrete and glass are both made using sand.

The Taj Mahal is a huge Indian tomb built from marble.

ENERGY FROM THE EARTH

The Earth's rocks, minerals and fossils contain energy which we can extract and use. Oil, gas and coal, which can be converted into heat and electricity, all come from the Earth. So do other forms of energy, such as nuclear energy.

This huge structure is the top part of an oil platform, which sticks out above the sea's surface. It contains equipment for processing the oil, and living quarters for the workers.

NORTH CORMORAN

Fossil fuels

Coal, oil and natural gas are fossil fuels. They are called this because, like fossils*, they form in the ground over many years from the bodies of dead plants and animals.

Coal is formed from trees and other plants that died thousands of years ago. Layers of sand and clay gradually settled on top of them, and compressed them slowly into thick, underground layers, or seams, of coal.

Oil is formed in the same way, but from the bodies of tiny sea creatures. It is found under the seabed, or underground (because some areas that were once sea are now land). Under certain conditions, natural gas is formed from dead plants and animals.

Extracting fuels

The coal we use comes from underground mines, or opencast mines, which are huge, open holes dug in the ground. To extract oil and gas, a drill, supported by a structure called a rig, bores a hole into the ground or seabed. Sometimes the fuel flows out naturally, but usually water is pumped into the hole to force the oil or gas out.

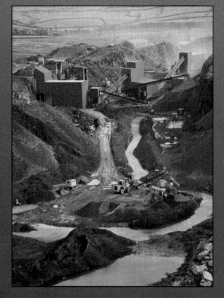

Coal being extracted from a mine at the surface of the ground, called an opencast mine

*Fossils, 21

Using fossil fuels

When a fossil fuel is burned, it releases energy, which is used to heat buildings and to run vehicle engines. In power stations, heat from fossil fuels is converted into electricity.

The world depends on fossil fuels. They provide more than three-quarters of the energy we use. But we use them up more quickly than they can form, so they are running out. In around 200 years, humans will need to get most of their energy in other ways.

As well as providing energy, oil is used to make plastic, which is made into thousands of things, from drinks bottles to polyester clothing.

Radiation

Some minerals found in the ground are radioactive. This means their atoms (the tiny particles they are made of) are unstable.

Instead of staying as they are, unstable minerals break up and send out particles or rays, known as radiation. As they break up, a type of energy called nuclear energy is released. Uranium, a metal, is the main radioactive mineral used to produce nuclear energy.

Like many metals, uranium doesn't exist naturally, but is found bonded together with other minerals in an ore*. After being mined from the ground, the uranium is extracted from the ore using chemical reactions.

This diagram shows how atoms of uranium produce nuclear energy.

A tiny particle called a neutron is fired at the uranium nucleus.

This is the nucleus, or middle, of a uranium atom.

The nucleus splits, giving off heat.

More neutrons fly off the nucleus and split other uranium atoms.

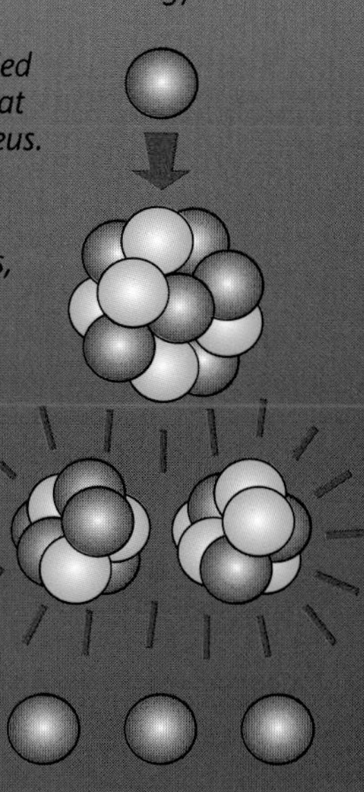

*Ore, 22

EARTHQUAKES AND VOLCANOES

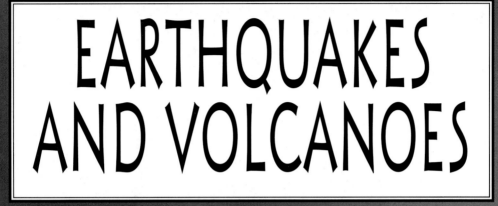

THE EXPLODING EARTH

A n erupting volcano is one of the most dramatic sights in the natural world. Bubbling hot lava spews out of a hole in the Earth's crust and engulfs the land. Ash, dust and poisonous gases pour into the air and chunks of rock are hurled high into the sky.

Volcanoes

Volcanoes erupt when red-hot molten rock, called magma, in the Earth's mantle rises towards the surface. Eventually it builds up enough pressure to burst through the Earth's crust. Once magma has reached the surface of the Earth it is called lava.

A cross-section through a cone volcano

Dust, ash and gases —

Crater ~ the hole at the top of a volcano

Volcanic bomb

Layers of volcanic ash ~ tiny particles of lava

Vent ~ the main pipe up the middle of a volcano

Dyke ~ a pipe leading from the vent to the surface

Magma chamber ~ place where magma collects below the Earth's crust

Growing

When a volcano erupts, the lava and ash it throws out eventually set as a solid layer of volcanic rock. As the layers build up, the volcano grows. Thick lava flows only a short way before setting, so it forms steep-sided cone volcanoes. Thinner lava flows further before setting hard, so it forms shield volcanoes that have gently sloping sides.

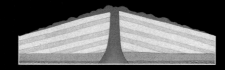

A cross-section through a shield volcano

Bombs and blocks

Volcanic bombs and blocks are thick lumps of molten lava which are blasted into the air as a volcano erupts. They start to cool and harden as they travel through the air. Blocks tend to be angular whereas bombs are more rounded.

Some blocks are the size of trucks.

As they twist through the air, some bombs form a "tail".

Tiny bombs shaped like drops form from very runny lava.

Dead or alive?

Volcanoes that erupt regularly are known as active volcanoes. Volcanoes that won't ever erupt again are called extinct volcanoes. Sometimes, people think a volcano is extinct when actually it is only dormant (sleeping). In 1973, on an island near Iceland, a volcano that was believed to be extinct erupted, destroying 300 buildings. It hadn't erupted for over 5,000 years.

Danger

Lava destroys everything it engulfs. But, because it usually flows quite slowly, it rarely kills people. There is more danger from the hot gas, bombs and ash which can sweep down a volcano's slopes at speeds of 200km/h (120 mph). In AD79, when Mount Vesuvius in Italy erupted, the people of Pompeii were wiped out by poisonous gas and ash.

A plaster cast made from the hollow of a body left in the ash in Pompeii.

VOLCANIC VARIATIONS

Most volcanoes occur at weak spots on the Earth's crust, where it is easiest for magma to burst through. Volcanoes erupt in different ways, depending on how thick their lava is.

Hot spots

Some volcanoes are found in the middle of plates. They may be caused by especially hot patches in the Earth's mantle, called hot spots. Scientists think that currents of extra-hot magma shoot up and burn through the Earth's crust to erupt on the surface.

Hot spot

Hot spots in the Earth's mantle may cause volcanoes in the middle of plates.

Volcanoes with runny lava, like this, erupt gently.

Spreading ridges

Whole mountain ranges of volcanoes can form at underwater boundaries where two plates are moving apart. These are called spreading ridges. As the plates move apart, magma from the mantle rises to the surface. Most of it solidifies on the edge of the plates to make new crust, but some works its way up to the seabed, where it erupts as volcanoes.

Spreading ridges form when plates move apart.

Rising magma

Subduction zones

Volcanoes also occur at subduction zones. These are places where two plates collide head on and one plate is pushed down beneath the other. As the plate is forced deeper and deeper underground, it begins to melt, forming magma. This newly formed magma rises up through cracks in the surface and explodes in a volcano.

At subduction zones, one plate is forced underground where it starts to melt.

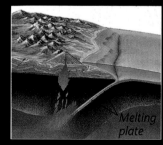

Melting plate

Thick or thin lava

Not all volcanoes erupt in the same way. Some throw clouds of ash high into the air, while others have a gentle lava fountain. The way a volcano erupts depends on the thickness and stickiness of the lava. The thicker and stickier the lava, the more gases are trapped within it. It is these gases that cause the build-up of pressure which makes a volcano erupt explosively.

When lava is thin and runny, gases can escape more easily. This makes an eruption less violent, because the gases can just bubble out of the top of the volcano. Many of the different types of eruptions are named after particular volcanoes that have erupted in that way.

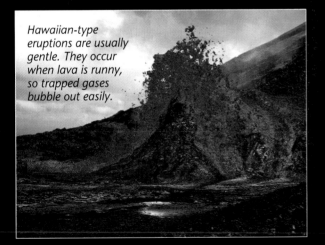

Hawaiian-type eruptions are usually gentle. They occur when lava is runny, so trapped gases bubble out easily.

Plinian-type eruptions are the most explosive. Trapped gases cause massive explosions as they escape and huge amounts of volcanic ash are thrown high into the air.

NATURAL HOT WATER

In areas where volcanoes are found, there are often other dramatic natural features and events as well as volcanic eruptions. Hot springs rich in minerals*, jets of steaming hot water which shoot into the air, and underwater chimneys which belch out black water can also be caused by volcanic activity.

Hot rock

In volcanic areas, when magma rises into the Earth's crust, it heats the rock around it. This rock might contain groundwater. Groundwater is rain or sea water which has seeped down into the Earth's crust through cracks in the surface. As the rock heats up, it heats the groundwater that comes into contact with it, producing a natural supply of hot water.

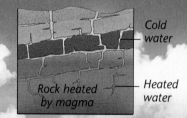

Cold water

Rock heated by magma

Heated water

Hot rock heats up groundwater.

Hot springs

Groundwater heated by hot rock sometimes bubbles to the surface as a hot, or thermal, spring. The water usually contains minerals which have been dissolved from the rock below. Minerals from the water often build up around the edge of the springs.

This is the Morning Glory pool, one of many hot springs in Yellowstone National Park, U.S.A. The park has over 10,000 features, such as hot springs and geysers, which have been caused by hot volcanic rock.

*Minerals, 21

32

Black smokers

Around volcanic mountain ranges under the sea, hot springs sometimes emerge through holes in the seabed called hydrothermal vents.

Some vents, called black smokers, look like chimneys and puff out plumes of hot, cloudy black water. The water is cloudy because of the minerals it has dissolved from the hot rock. As minerals are deposited around the vent, the sides of the chimney build up. Some unusual creatures live near black smokers, such as tubeworms and blind spider crabs. They feed on bacteria which live on the minerals given out by the vents.

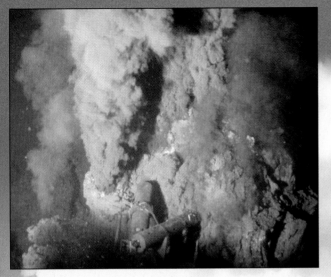

Black smokers form on the seabed and puff out clouds of hot, black water. Some are as tall as 6m (20ft).

Geysers

A geyser is a jet of hot water and steam which shoots into the air from a hole in the ground. Geysers occur when heated groundwater gets trapped in a network of cracks under the Earth's surface. Because the water is trapped, it continues to heat up until it boils and forms steam. The pressure builds up until it forces the water to find a way out of the ground. This results in occasional bursts of hot water.

"Old Faithful" is a geyser in Yellowstone National Park, U.S.A. A fountain of hot water like this spurts out once every hour or so.

VOLCANIC ISLANDS

A volcanic island called White Island, off the coast of New Zealand

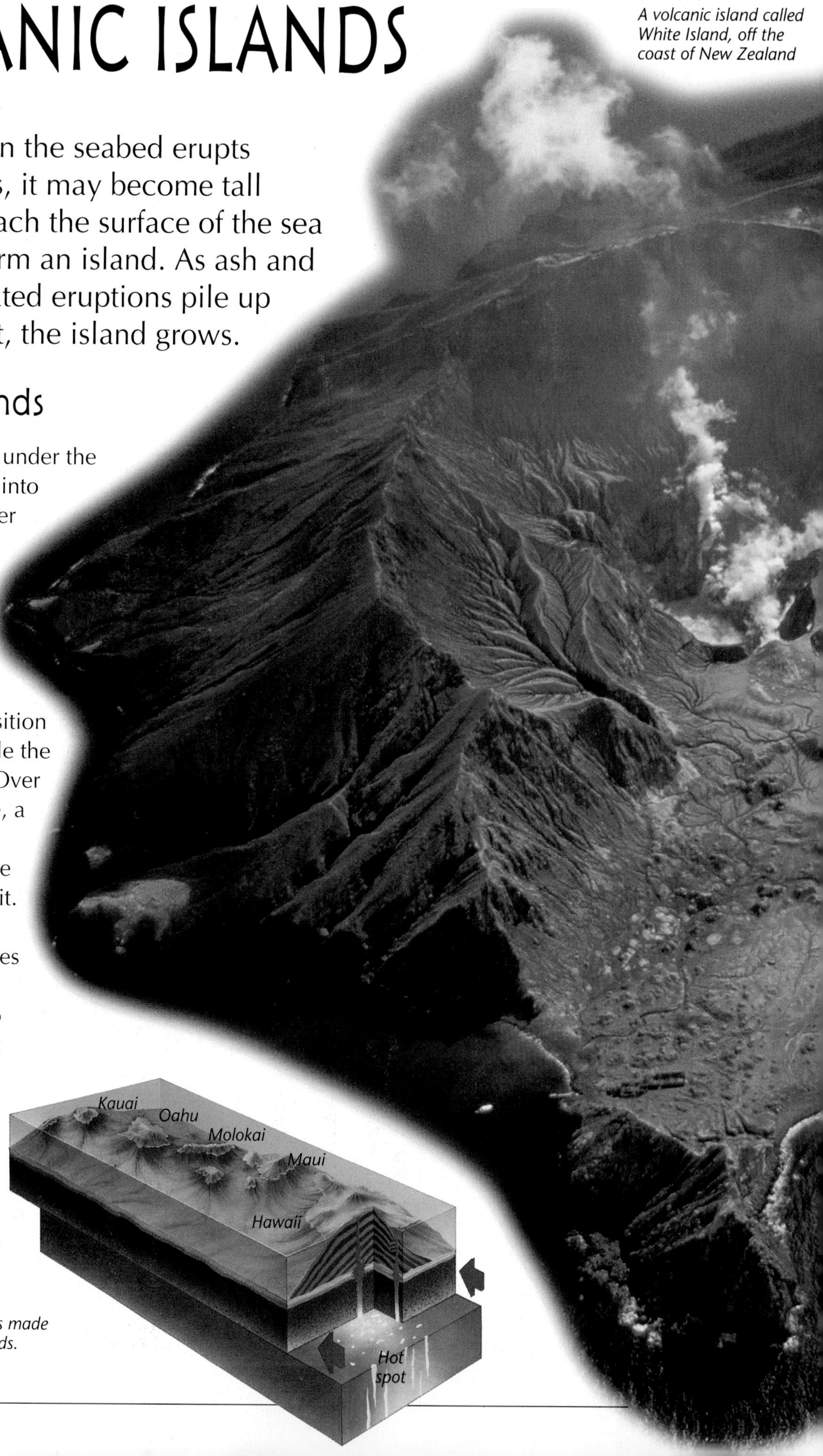

If a volcano on the seabed erupts enough times, it may become tall enough to reach the surface of the sea and begin to form an island. As ash and lava from repeated eruptions pile up around the vent, the island grows.

Hot spot islands

Hot spot volcanoes* under the sea sometimes grow into volcanic islands. Over thousands of years, a hot spot can produce a chain of volcanic islands. Scientists think that hot spots remain in a fixed position inside the Earth, while the crust above moves. Over a long period of time, a volcanic island is carried away from the hot spot that caused it.

When an island moves away from a hot spot, the volcano becomes extinct as it loses its supply of magma. A new volcano then forms on the part of the plate lying above the hot spot. Eventually a chain of islands is formed.

The Hawaiian island chain is made up of hot spot volcanic islands.

*Hot spots, 30

Island arcs

Curved chains of volcanic islands, known as island arcs, sometimes form above subduction zones* where magma rises through cracks in the seabed. Scientists are not sure why they form an arc, but it may be connected with the way the plates move, or the spherical shape of the Earth.

An island is born

This picture shows steam and ash billowing from Surtsey, a volcanic island near Iceland.

In 1963, fishermen off the coast of Iceland saw smoke rising from the sea. They thought it must be a boat on fire. In fact, it wasn't smoke, but ash and steam from a volcano just below the water's surface.

During the next four years, the volcano erupted many times. As it emerged above the water, the eruptions became more explosive as water pressure decreased. Lava and ash built up, until eventually they formed a volcanic island. The island was named Surtsey after Surt, the Nordic giant of fire.

Black beaches

Some volcanic islands have black sandy beaches. This is because they are formed from basalt lava which is black. When the lava runs down to meet the sea, it cools instantly. The change in temperature makes the lava shatter into tiny pieces which form the grains of sand.

A black sandy beach in Tahiti

*Subduction zones, 30

LIVING WITH VOLCANOES

Despite the danger that active volcanoes present, many people choose to live on their slopes. Scientists have found ways to help predict when eruptions will happen, so they are sometimes able to warn those at risk.

Monitoring volcanoes

Before a volcano erupts, the ground may change shape. This kind of change can be measured by instruments such as tiltmeters and geodimeters. The ground may also begin to tremble. This is known as volcanic tremor. It can be detected by seismometers.

Such instruments were used to monitor the Mount St. Helens volcano, Washington, U.S.A., in early 1980. They recorded a bulge swelling by 1.5m (5ft) per day. The area around the volcano was evacuated shortly before it erupted.

A group of experts monitoring the Mount St. Helens volcano were in a plane flying over it when the volcano began to shudder. This photograph of the eruption was taken as the pilot turned the plane to escape the blast.

The area around Mount St. Helens after the eruption. Despite the evacuation of the area, 61 people died.

A bulge on the side of Mount St. Helens swelled to 90m (295ft) before a massive eruption blasted away the side of the volcano.

Using volcanoes

Although volcanoes are usually a destructive force, they can also be put to productive uses.

The ash from volcanoes contains minerals which make soil very fertile. As a result, the land around volcanoes is very good for farming. This is one of the reasons why people choose to live in such dangerous places.

Engineers have discovered how to use the heat energy in volcanic rock to produce electricity. When groundwater seeps into the cracks in volcanic rock, it gets hot. (Sometimes cracks are created artificially to produce the same effect.) The hot water is then pumped up to the surface where it is converted into steam. The steam is used to turn machines called turbines which make electricity.

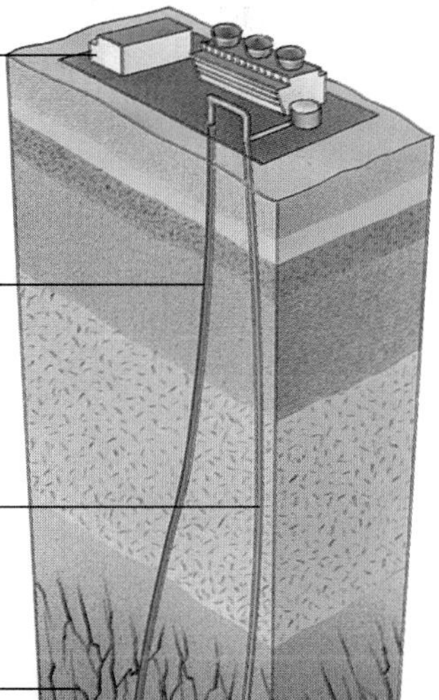

A power station produces electricity.

Hot water is pumped to the surface to turn turbines.

Cold water is pumped into the ground.

Artificial cracks

At some power stations, cold water is pumped into specially-made cracks in volcanic rock.

EARTHQUAKE EFFECTS

An earthquake is a sudden release of energy which makes the ground tremble. The effects of a large earthquake can be devastating: the ground lurches violently and buildings sway from side to side, or may even collapse. However, earthquakes only occur in certain parts of the world and most earthquakes are not felt by people at all.

An apartment block in San Francisco, U.S.A., which has been damaged by an earthquake

Damaging effects

Earthquakes cause most damage when they occur in large towns and cities. During severe earthquakes, buildings and bridges collapse, and cracks called fissures may appear in the ground. There are also threats from hazards such as fire and flooding. These may be caused when underground gas pipes or water pipes crack during an earthquake.

The power of earthquakes

Over 800,000 earthquakes occur each year, but only around 1,000 of these cause significant damage. Their power and effects are measured by seismologists, scientists who study earthquakes.

There are two scales for measuring earthquakes: the Richter scale and the Mercalli scale. The Richter scale measures the power of vibrations called seismic waves, that travel through the ground when an earthquake happens. These vibrations are registered using a device called a seismometer. Then a chart of the vibrations, known as a seismogram, is produced.

Earthquakes are rated between 1 and 10 on the Richter scale. With each step up the scale, the energy released is about 30 times greater than at the step below.

This is a device called a seismometer, which is used to measure ground vibrations.

This shows the devastation caused by an earthquake in Maharashtra, India, in 1993.

Mercalli scale

The Mercalli scale rates earthquakes from I to XII according to the effects of the shaking, including the damage caused in different places. It is based on information from eyewitnesses.

These pictures show how earthquakes are rated using the Mercalli scale. Ratings below IV indicate very slight vibrations.

IV
People indoors may notice plates and windows start to rattle.

V
Small objects move and liquids in glasses and bowls splash around.

VI
Books and ornaments fall off shelves. Vibrations are felt indoors and outdoors.

VII
Walls crack and tiles and bricks fall from buildings.

VIII
Some weaker buildings collapse.

IX+
Many larger buildings collapse.

HOW EARTHQUAKES HAPPEN

Earthquakes are most common near plate boundaries*. The movement of the plates causes stress to build up in certain areas of rock. When this stress is suddenly released, the surrounding rock vibrates, causing an earthquake.

Fault lines

Earthquakes occur along cracks in the Earth's crust called faults. Faults can be tiny fractures or long cracks stretching over vast distances. They occur when plates slide against each other, causing the rock to be twisted, stretched or squeezed until it splits. Boundaries where plates slide past each other in the same or in opposite directions are called conservative margins.

San Francisco

The North American plate moves 1cm a year.

San Andreas fault

Los Angeles

The Pacific plate moves 6cm a year.

San Diego

Mexico

Earthquakes regularly occur along the San Andreas fault, along the west coast of America. These plates slide in the same direction, but move at different speeds.

This diagram shows how some plates slide past each other in opposite directions.

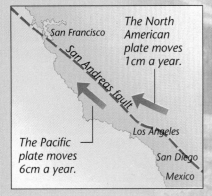

An overhead view of the San Andreas fault

Releasing energy

If the jagged edges along a fault become jammed, energy builds up as the two edges strain against one another. Eventually, the stress becomes so great that one side is suddenly forced to give way, causing a jerking movement. The energy that has built up is released, making the surrounding rock vibrate in an earthquake.

A fault running through rock

Energy builds up at the point where the rocks become jammed.

*Plate boundaries, 18

The focus

The point where the rock gives way is called the focus. This is where an earthquake starts. The focus is usually about 5-15km (3-9 miles) underground. The point on the surface directly above the focus is called the epicentre. Seismic waves travel outwards from the focus in all directions. The strength of an earthquake depends on the amount of energy released. However, waves from even a small earthquake can be detected on the other side of the world.

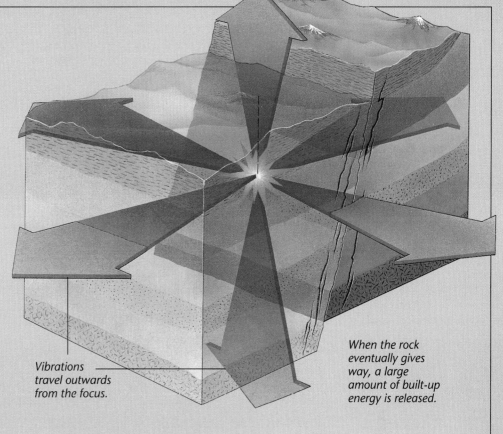

Vibrations travel outwards from the focus.

When the rock eventually gives way, a large amount of built-up energy is released.

Seismic waves

Seismic waves are at their strongest nearest the focus and become weaker as they travel out. There are different types of seismic waves, each of which makes the rock it travels through vibrate in a different way.

Different types of seismic waves travel by distorting rock in different ways.

→ Direction of waves

↔ Vibrations of the rock particles as the waves pass through

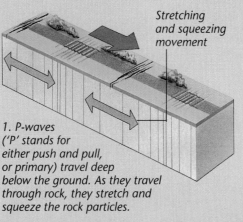

Stretching and squeezing movement

1. P-waves ('P' stands for either push and pull, or primary) travel deep below the ground. As they travel through rock, they stretch and squeeze the rock particles.

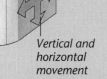

2. S-waves ('S' stands for either shake or secondary) make the rock move up and down and from side to side. They travel deep underground.

Vertical and horizontal movement

Circular movement

3. L-waves ('L' stands for long) only travel along the surface. Most earthquake damage is caused by this type of wave.

Aftershocks

Sometimes, not all of the energy that has built up is released during an earthquake. This may mean that after the main earthquake there are smaller tremors, known as aftershocks, as the remaining energy is released. Small amounts of energy may also be released before an earthquake occurs. This produces tremors known as foreshocks.

EARTHQUAKE SAFETY

B y monitoring faults, scientists can sometimes predict when and where earthquakes are likely to occur. This means that they can take steps to limit the damage caused by an earthquake or even prevent an earthquake from happening.

Seismic gaps

Stress that builds up at fault boundaries is often released gradually by slow movement known as fault creep. Earthquakes are less likely to happen in areas where fault creep occurs, because stress is being released. They are most likely to occur at sections of a fault where there has been no movement for many years. These sections are known as seismic gaps.

A recent earthquake has caused stress to be released.

Seismic gap

Area where fault creep is occurring

By identifying seismic gaps, scientists can carefully monitor areas where earthquakes are most likely to occur.

Monitoring faults

If the surface of the Earth suddenly starts to tilt, it may be a sign that an earthquake is about to happen. Devices called tiltmeters can measure tiny changes in the level of the ground.

Horizontal movement along faults can be monitored using lasers. A laser beam is bounced off a reflector, which then reflects it back. A computer records the time it takes the beam to travel this distance. If the time changes, it shows that movement has taken place.

Scientists use lasers like these to detect ground movements. They can detect shifts as slight as 1mm (0.04in).

Preventing earthquakes

Earthquakes can be prevented by releasing jammed plates before too much stress builds up. This can be done by conducting a small explosion to shift the plates. Alternatively, drilling deep holes and injecting water into rocks reduces friction, enabling smoother movement along a fault.

Keeping safe

During an earthquake, if you are indoors, the safest place to be is under a solid table or desk. You should cover your eyes to protect them from flying glass and hold on tightly to the leg of the table. If you are outside, it's better to be in an open space, away from buildings, trees and power lines.

Animal instincts

Animals have sometimes been reported as behaving strangely shortly before an earthquake. For example, shortly before an earthquake in Haicheng, China, in 1975, snakes that had been hibernating emerged unexpectedly. Scientists think this may be because animals' highly developed senses can detect slight vibrations, changes in electrical currents in rocks, or the release of gases. In San Francisco, U.S.A, zoo animals are monitored in case the way they behave provides clues that an earthquake is about to happen.

If animals become unusually agitated, it may be a clue that an earthquake is about to happen.

Safe buildings

In areas where there is a high risk of earthquakes happening, more buildings are being designed so that minimum damage is caused if there is an earthquake. The foundations of some buildings are constructed to absorb vibrations and reduce the effects of shaking. Steel frames can be used to strengthen buildings, so that a building may sway but will not collapse when the ground trembles.

The Transamerica skyscraper in San Francisco, U.S.A., is designed to withstand earth tremors.

GIANT WAVES

An earthquake or a volcanic eruption under the sea or near the coast can cause giant waves called tsunami. These waves surge across the sea in all directions. Just before a tsunami crashes onto the shore, it slows down suddenly and may swell to an enormous height.

A tsunami hit Papua New Guinea in 1998, causing incredible devastation. This is a still from a video taken there. It shows steel roofing wrapped around a tree by the force of the wave.

Tsunami

Tsunami begin when an earthquake or volcano causes ground movement on the seabed or near the sea. This jolt shifts the water, causing waves to form. Out at sea, tsunami are a similar height to ordinary waves, although the distance between the top, or crest, of one tsunami and the next can be more than 100km (62 miles). What makes tsunami so dangerous is their speed. They race across the sea at speeds of up to 800km/h (500mph). As a tsunami reaches the shore, the friction of the seabed against the water acts like a brake, forcing it to slow down suddenly. The height of the tsunami increases to form a wall of water which towers above the shore and then crashes down, rushing inland and flooding the coast.

Tsunami travel out rapidly in all directions from the place where they initially form.

An underwater earthquake or volcanic eruption displaces the seabed.

Tsunami swell to great heights before crashing onto the shore.

Tsunami warning system

Most tsunami occur in the Pacific Ocean. For this reason, there are observation stations throughout the Pacific to monitor earthquakes. If an earthquake is large enough to generate tsunami, warnings are issued to coastal towns, so that they can prepare for it. Tide stations along the coast then monitor the arrival of the tsunami.

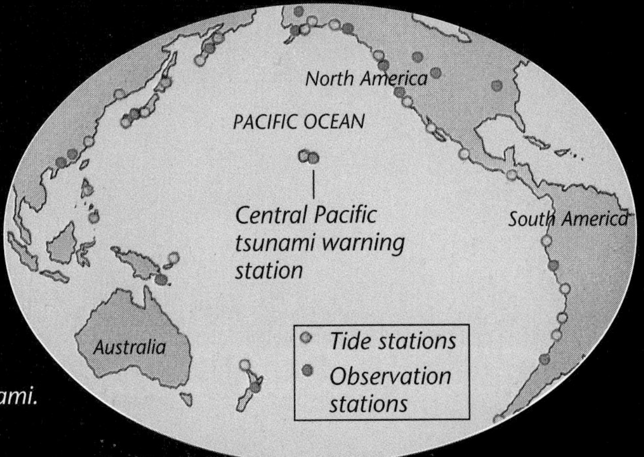

Observation and tide stations in the Pacific monitor tsunami.

North America

PACIFIC OCEAN

Central Pacific tsunami warning station

South America

Australia

Tide stations

Observation stations

Tsunami look like a huge wall of water. They can reach heights of up to 50m (165ft).

Autumn in the Cache National Forest, Idaho, U.S.A.

CLIMATE

THE EARTH'S ATMOSPHERE

Surrounding the Earth is a blanket of gases which make up its atmosphere. The atmosphere contains the air we need to breathe. It also affects weather and climate and protects us from extremes of temperature and from the Sun's harmful rays.

The atmosphere's structure

The gases surrounding the Earth are held by gravity, a force which attracts things to Earth. The atmosphere is divided into layers according to the temperature of these gases. The diagram below shows the different layers.

This diagram shows some of the layers in the Earth's atmosphere. The outermost layer, the exosphere, is not marked; it is around 400km (250 miles) from Earth.

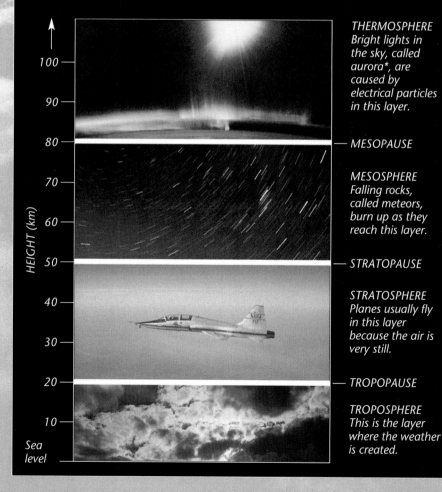

HEIGHT (km)

100 —
90 —
80 —
70 —
60 —
50 —
40 —
30 —
20 —
10 —
Sea level

THERMOSPHERE
Bright lights in the sky, called aurora*, are caused by electrical particles in this layer.

— MESOPAUSE

MESOSPHERE
Falling rocks, called meteors, burn up as they reach this layer.

— STRATOPAUSE

STRATOSPHERE
Planes usually fly in this layer because the air is very still.

— TROPOPAUSE

TROPOSPHERE
This is the layer where the weather is created.

The troposphere

The troposphere is the layer of the atmosphere nearest to the Earth's surface. As well as a mixture of gases, this layer contains clouds, dust and pollution. It extends to between 10km (6 miles) and 20km (12 miles) from the Earth. Temperatures are high near the Earth because the air is heated from below by the Earth's surface, which is warmed by the Sun. Higher up, the air is thinner and can't hold as much heat, so temperatures decrease.

The troposphere is the layer where the weather is produced. It gets its name from the Greek word *tropos* which means "a turn". This is because the air there is constantly circulating*.

The stratosphere

The upper limit of the stratosphere is around 50km (30 miles) from the Earth's surface. When you fly in a plane, you fly in this layer, just above the clouds.

The stratosphere contains a concentration of ozone gas which absorbs ultraviolet rays from the Sun. This causes the stratosphere to heat up. This layer of ozone gas is very important, as it helps to shield the Earth from harmful ultraviolet rays, which can cause skin cancer and damage to the eyes.

The mesosphere

The mesosphere reaches a height of around 80km (50 miles). Temperatures here are the coolest in the atmosphere because the mesosphere contains no ozone, dust or clouds, which absorb energy from the Sun. It is hottest at the bottom due to the warmer stratosphere layer below.

The thermosphere

Temperatures in the thermosphere can be extremely high, reaching up to 1500°C (2732°F). This is because there is a high proportion of a gas called atomic oxygen. This absorbs ultraviolet rays from the Sun in the same way that ozone does.

The ozone layer

The layer of ozone gas in the stratosphere is being damaged by chemicals called chlorofluorocarbons (CFCs), which are used in some spray cans and refrigerators. At certain times of year, a hole in the ozone layer appears over Antarctica, and in other areas the ozone layer becomes very thin. This damage means that more of these harmful ultraviolet rays reach the Earth's surface.

The bright pink areas in this picture show a hole in the layer of ozone gas over Antarctica.

When you fly in a plane in the stratosphere you can often see the clouds in the troposphere below.

AIR AND OCEAN CURRENTS

As the Sun heats the Earth, it causes air and water to move around in the form of currents. As particles of air and water are heated, they expand and rise and then cool and fall, producing patterns of circulating air and water, which are crucial in determining climate.

The circular shapes on the satellite image in the background are called spiral eddies. They are swirls of water which have separated from the main band, or current, of water.

Moving air

The air around us is constantly pushing in every direction. The force that it exerts as it does is known as atmospheric pressure.

The movement of air is affected by temperature. The Sun heats up the land and oceans, which in turn heat the air directly above in the troposphere*. As the air is heated, it rises and moves off, leaving behind an area of low pressure. When the air cools, it sinks down on the Earth's surface in a different area, causing high pressure.

Because the Sun doesn't heat up the world evenly, there are differences of pressure. Where there is a difference, air rushes from high to low pressure areas in order to even out the pressure. This moving air is wind. As the air moves, the spinning of the Earth causes it to be deflected into fast spirals. This deflection is known as the Coriolis effect*.

Global winds

Air is constantly circulating between the tropics and the poles as global winds. Warm air flows from the tropics* and pushes out the cold air at the poles, which then flows back towards the tropics. The Westerlies and trade winds are examples of global winds.

Global winds form because areas near the Equator receive more heat from the Sun than other areas. As the air is heated, it rises and spreads out. When it cools, it sinks at around 30° north and south of the Equator, causing pressure at the Earth's surface to increase. This forces the air outwards in the direction of both the Equator and the poles.

A satellite image showing winds over the Pacific Ocean. The tiny arrows overlaying the image show the direction of the winds.

Moving water

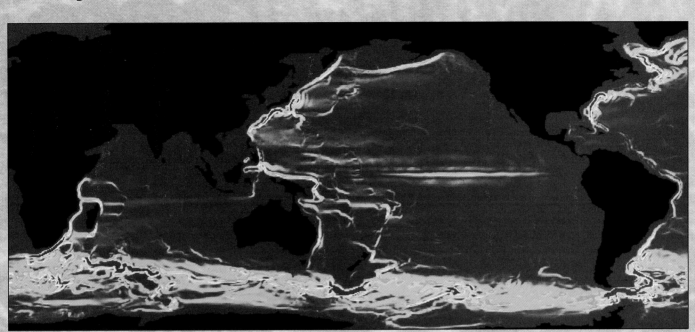

This image shows ocean currents around the world. The red areas are fast currents and the light blue areas are slow currents.

Ocean currents are wide bands of water, like rivers that flow in the world's oceans. They sweep around the oceans, moving water between hot and cold places.

Just as heat from the Sun causes the movement of air, it also causes the movement of water in the form of currents. However, in the oceans, the temperature difference between the poles and the

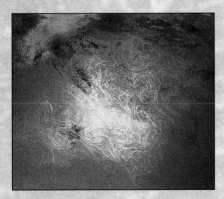

A satellite picture of part of the Gulf Stream, a current of water that flows in the Atlantic Ocean.

Equator is greater than it is on land. Near the Equator, the Sun's rays penetrate far below the ocean's surface. At the poles, the Sun's rays hit the water at a shallow angle. This causes the water to act like a mirror, reflecting rather than absorbing the Sun's rays.

Effects of currents

Currents vary in temperature and move at different speeds. If a current is much warmer or cooler than the surrounding water, it can dramatically affect the climates of the coastal areas that it flows near. A current called the Gulf Stream, which runs between the Gulf of Mexico and Europe (where it becomes the North Atlantic Drift), brings a mild climate to northwest Europe. The Labrador current

is a cold current which runs from the Arctic Ocean along the northeast coast of North America, bringing a cold climate to Newfoundland.

El Niño

The incredible effect that the warming of the ocean can have on weather and climate is illustrated by a phenomenon known as El Niño. Every few years, a current of water in the Pacific, off the northwest coast of South America, suddenly becomes warmer. Scientists are not sure why this happens, but it sets in motion a chain of climatic changes, including floods, droughts and severe storms.

NATURAL CYCLES

Some substances, such as nitrogen and carbon, are constantly changing form as they move around in huge cycles. This exchange of substances is essential to life on Earth. The air, land, water, plants, animals, and even your own body, all form a part of these cycles.

This magnified part of a pea plant contains bacteria which convert nitrogen from the air into a form the plant can use.

Keeping a balance

Living things take in substances such as oxygen, nitrogen, carbon and water from the world around them through food, soil and air. They use them to live and grow. When a plant or animal dies and decays, its body is broken down and gases are released into the air. The cycle continues, with these substances being used again and again. This process maintains the balance of gases in the air.

The nitrogen cycle

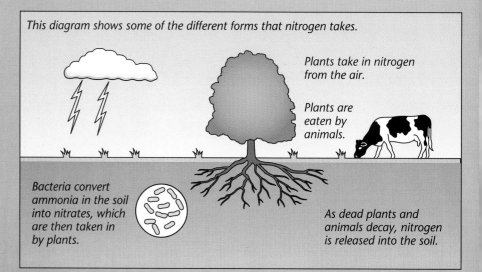

This diagram shows some of the different forms that nitrogen takes.

Plants take in nitrogen from the air.

Plants are eaten by animals.

Bacteria convert ammonia in the soil into nitrates, which are then taken in by plants.

As dead plants and animals decay, nitrogen is released into the soil.

Nitrogen (chemical symbol ~ N) makes up 78% of the air. Plants and animals need it for growth. Plants take in nitrogen from the air and the soil. Bacteria convert the substance into a form the plants can use. Animals obtain nitrogen by eating plants or by eating animals that have eaten plants. When plants and animals die and decay, fungi and bacteria break down their remains and nitrogen is released back into the soil.

This dung beetle is feeding on animal dung. Insects like this help to break down plant and animal matter.

One form that carbon can take is charcoal, as shown here. Charcoal can be burned as a fuel. When it is burned, it gives out carbon dioxide.

The carbon cycle

Carbon forms part of the gases in the air, mainly as carbon dioxide (chemical symbol ~ CO_2), which is a compound of carbon and oxygen. Plants take in CO_2 from the air and use it to make food. At night, they give out CO_2.

Animals obtain carbon by eating plants. They release carbon in their waste and when they breathe out. CO_2 is also released when plants and animals die and decay. Carbon can be stored in the form of fossilized remains. Eventually these form fossil fuels* such as coal and oil, which release CO_2 when burned.

Upsetting cycles

Left alone, these cycles create a natural balance of gases. However, human activities are interfering with this balance by adding waste and pollution to the atmosphere. The effects of human disruption on the carbon cycle are described on pages 54 to 55.

One of the major factors that affects the nitrogen cycle is farming. When farmers harvest crops, they remove plants which have taken in nitrates from the soil. Because the plants are not allowed to decay naturally, the nitrogen is not returned to the soil, and the cycle is broken.

The algae in this canal is thriving because of excess nitrates running into it from fertilizer used on nearby farmland.

Farmers often use chemical fertilizers* to replace nitrates in soil. But this can also upset the balance, as it's difficult to judge the right amount of nitrates. If too much is added, it can seep through the soil into rivers, where it can affect plants and animals.

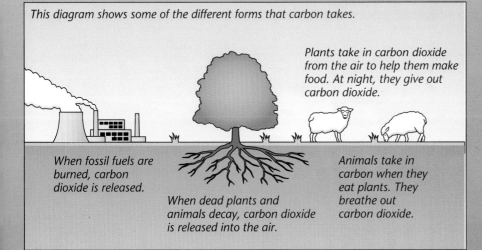

This diagram shows some of the different forms that carbon takes.

Plants take in carbon dioxide from the air to help them make food. At night, they give out carbon dioxide.

When fossil fuels are burned, carbon dioxide is released.

When dead plants and animals decay, carbon dioxide is released into the air.

Animals take in carbon when they eat plants. They breathe out carbon dioxide.

*Fertilizer, 114; fossil fuels, 24

GLOBAL WARMING

Some of the gases in the atmosphere help to keep the Earth warm. They trap heat from the Sun in the same way that a greenhouse traps heat. This process is known as the greenhouse effect. But, as these gases increase, the Earth could be becoming too warm.

A magnified picture of pollen from the ragwort plant. As the Earth warms up, pollen from plants may increase. This could cause problems for people with allergies.

Greenhouse gases

The Earth's surface absorbs some of the heat from the Sun, but the rest is bounced back into the atmosphere. Most of it escapes into space, but some is trapped in the atmosphere by gases known as greenhouse gases. The main greenhouse gases are carbon dioxide and water in the form of clouds. As the amount of greenhouse gases increases, more heat is trapped.

Most greenhouse gases occur naturally, but industrial processes and other pollution are increasing the amount of greenhouse gases in the atmosphere. Scientists think that this may be causing the Earth to become warmer. This process is known as global warming.

Plants are important for the balance of greenhouse gases because they take in carbon dioxide.

Balance of gases

Whenever we burn oil, coal or wood, carbon dioxide is released. For example, when forests are burned to make room for farming, they release carbon dioxide. This also reduces the number of plants available to absorb carbon dioxide, upsetting the natural balance of the carbon cycle*. Factories, power stations and cars also give out pollution which may contribute to global warming.

Huge roads like this one are useful for car drivers. But the pollution from cars could be contributing to global warming.

cArthur Blvd
n Wayne Airport
NEXT EXIT

Venice, Italy, is a city built on over 100 tiny islands in the Lagoon of Venice. If the sea level rises, it may eventually disappear under the sea.

Rising sea level

As temperatures rise, so will the sea level. This will eventually result in the flooding of low-lying areas. Scientists estimate that the sea level is rising at a rate of 1-2mm (0.04-0.08ins) each year. It may rise by a further 0.25-1m (0.8-3.3ft) by the year 2100. There are two main reasons for the increased volume of water. Firstly, as the oceans heat up, the water expands. The sea level rises because the water is taking up more space. Secondly, the higher temperatures may cause glaciers and polar icecaps to melt. This water will then flood into the sea.

Changing climate

If temperatures rise, climates all over the world will be affected. Scientists predict that the average temperature will increase by around 2°C (35.6°F) in the next century. The effect this will have is not known. Some areas may become warmer and drier, and others wetter. There may also be an increase in extreme weather such as strong winds and rainstorms.

Changes in climates will also affect the habitats* of plants and animals. This could help some species to thrive, while others may be forced to move in search of food and water if they are to survive.

Shifting the balance

People have already begun to take steps to reduce the emission of gases that contribute to global warming. The main ways that this can be achieved are by looking at alternative energy sources and reducing pollution levels.

*Carbon cycle, 53; habitats, 100

WORLD CLIMATES

The long-term or typical pattern of
weather in a particular area is known
as its climate. Climates vary enormously
in different parts of the world. They determine
the character of an area, affecting the plants,
animals and people that live there.

*This map of the Earth's surface contains
information from several different
satellites*. It shows some
of the main climate
types around
the world.*

*Maple trees grow
in temperate
regions, which
have lots of
vegetation.*

*Temperate and tropical
regions are green. They
contain lots of vegetation.*

*Tropical grasslands and deserts
are yellow and brown. They are
dry, with little vegetation.*

*Snowy regions are light blue
or white. The swirling white
masses are clouds.*

Climate types

Areas can be grouped into
several main climate types,
such as polar, temperate and
tropical. These are also
known as biomes*. The most
important factor in
determining an area's climate
is its latitude*, because this
affects the amount of heat

received from the Sun. This in
turn has a crucial effect on the
vegetation and animals which
give each climate zone its
distinctive characteristics.

The map above shows how
areas at the same latitude
share broadly similar

climates. The different climate
zones are described in more
detail on the following pages.

Other factors, such as height
and distance from the ocean,
are also very important in
determining the climate of a
particular area.

*Biomes, 101; latitude, 10; satellites, 11

High places

Mountain regions have a different climate from the surrounding lowland areas. It frequently rains and snows, as clouds are forced to rise to pass over the mountains. The tops of many high mountains are covered in snow for most of the year.

Temperatures in mountain regions can be extremely cold because the air is thinner higher up and so it can't hold as much heat. In addition, the area of land heating the surrounding air decreases, making it cooler.

Land and sea

Climate is affected by the oceans. Places near the sea have a maritime climate, a milder and wetter climate than areas further inland. Temperatures there are not usually as extreme as inland areas of the same latitude. This is because ocean temperatures change less than land temperatures and this affects the climate of areas nearby. The climates of inland areas are known as continental climates.

The moose lives in forests in cool temperate regions.

Land surfaces

Different land surfaces absorb the Sun's rays differently. Light surfaces, such as snow-covered land or deserts, reflect the Sun's rays, whereas dense forests and dark soils absorb them. Where a higher proportion of the rays is reflected, clouds are less likely to form. This means that areas with lighter land surfaces will have less rainfall. Clouds also reflect the Sun's rays, affecting the amount of energy reaching the Earth's surface.

RAINFORESTS

This is a tropical rainforest in Bali, Indonesia. The tallest trees tower above the canopy. They are called emergents.

In the tropics*, it rains nearly every day and is hot throughout the year. Large areas are covered in thick, lush forests called tropical rainforests.

Rainy places

Tropical rainforests receive more than 4,000mm (160in) of rain each year. The intense heat causes water to evaporate quickly, making the air very moist, or humid.

Inside the rainforests it is dark and damp. As trees compete to reach the light, they grow quickly, spreading out their branches to absorb the light. Their leaves form a thick green canopy which blocks out most of the Sun's rays.

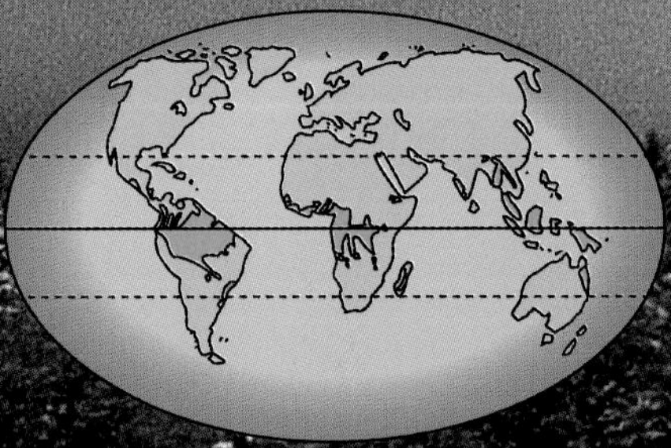

This map show where the tropical rainforests are.

In places the canopy can be up to 7m (23ft) thick. The area between the canopy and the ground is called the understorey.

*Tropics, 146

Rainforest people

Many traditional groups, or tribes, of people living in tropical rainforests survive by hunting animals and gathering plants, or by small-scale farming. However, recently other settlers have moved into these areas for commercial reasons. They chop down trees and burn them in order to clear land, which is then used for growing crops or grazing cattle.

These rainforest trees are being burned to create space for farming.

Animal life

Rainforests are home to over half the world's plant and animal species. Different kinds of animals have adapted to living at different levels in the rainforest. Many animals live in the branches of trees. They need to be good at climbing and able to move easily from tree to tree by swinging, jumping or gliding.

On the forest floor, the tangled vegetation makes it difficult for some animals to move around. The larger animals tend to be sturdy so that they can easily force their way through. There are also many insects on the forest floor.

Colugos, or flying lemurs, climb trees to eat leaves and fruit. They use the flaps of skin between their arms and legs to help them glide between trees.

Forests in danger

Every year, huge areas of rainforest are chopped down or burned. The disappearance of so many trees affects the balance of gases in the atmosphere. This may cause an increase in global warming*. Due to the destruction of their natural habitat, many rainforest plants and animals have died out and many others are endangered.

Golden lion tamarins are an endangered species of monkey.

*Global warming, 54

TROPICAL GRASSLANDS

The tropical grasslands are flat, open plains in the central parts of continents. They occur between 5° and 15° north and south of the Equator and get their name from the grasses that make up the majority of the vegetation.

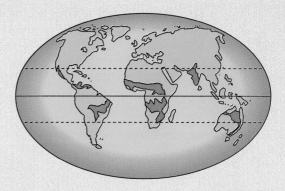

This map shows where the tropical grasslands are.

Acacia trees in the Taragire National Park, Tanzania, Africa. Acacias are among the few trees that can survive in the dry tropical grasslands.

Two seasons

The tropical grasslands have two seasons: a dry season, when the vegetation is dry and brown, and a rainy season, when the grasses become tall and green.

The rainy season in an area occurs when the Sun is directly overhead and the trade winds* meet there. As the warm moist air is forced to rise, it rains heavily. When the Sun is no longer directly overhead, the point where the trade winds meet shifts and the dry season begins. The trade winds are dry because they have already shed any moisture on the coast.

Vegetation

Only a few trees grow in the tropical grasslands, for example the acacia tree whose thick trunk is resistant to the fires that sometimes rage during the dry season. However, there are around 8000 species of grasses, which are well adapted to surviving the dry season. Their long roots can reach out in search of the little water that is available.

*Trade winds, 50

Grassland animals

The tropical grasslands are home to large numbers of herbivores (plant-eating animals). These attract large hunting animals, such as lions and cheetahs, that feed on them. Because the land is so exposed, many animals live in large groups, so that some animals can watch out for predators while others feed or rest.

Some of the fastest animals, such as cheetahs, gazelles and ostriches, live in grasslands. Speed is important for survival, both for the hunters and the hunted. With so few hiding places, a hunt for food often results in a chase.

During the dry season, wildebeest move away, or migrate, to find food and water. Many thousands of wildebeest migrate together for protection.

Cheetahs are the fastest land mammals, reaching speeds of up to 110kph (68mph).

The tsetse fly

Many grassland areas are now used for farming. However the largest grasslands, in Africa, are almost untouched. This is because of a parasite, carried by an insect called the tsetse fly, which infects humans and animals. In humans, it causes sleeping sickness, the effects of which are sluggishness, fever and sometimes death. In animals, it causes a similar disease called nagana.

A close-up of a tsetse fly feeding on a human arm.

MONSOONS

At certain times of year, some areas of the tropics have a period of torrential rain known as a monsoon. The heavy rain can cause severe flooding, but people rely on the rain for survival. In fact, the start of the rainy season is often welcomed with celebrations.

Three seasons

Monsoons occur in certain parts of the tropics, particularly in Southeast Asia. Monsoon regions have three seasons ~ a long cool dry season, a hot humid season when the land is very dry, and a rainy season when there are thunderstorms on most days.

During the rainy season, it rains very heavily and there are strong winds. You can see how strong the winds are by the way the trees are blowing.

Changing winds

The word *monsoon* comes from an Arabic word which means "season". It refers to the rainy season and to the seasonal winds that cause it. During the dry season, the land is cooler than the ocean, and so dry winds blow from the land to the ocean. The rainy season occurs when the Sun is almost directly overhead. The land is hotter than the ocean, so moist winds rush in from the ocean. As the winds rise and cool, they shed their moisture as heavy rain.

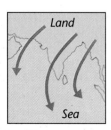

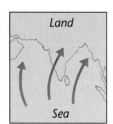

In the dry season, winds blow from the land to the sea.

In the rainy season, moist winds rush in from the sea.

Farming

Around a quarter of the world's people live in monsoon areas. Many of them rely on growing their own food. The main crops are rice and tea, which grow well in wet conditions.

Rice in particular needs lots of water to grow. The seedlings are planted during the monsoon season in flooded fields called paddy fields. Rice is an important food for many poor nations, because it can be grown cheaply and in large quantities. Too little rain in the monsoon season can be disastrous, resulting in crop failure and possibly famine.

When trees are cut down for wood and to clear space for farming, it means that there are no more roots to hold the soil* together. In monsoon regions, this can cause problems, because heavy rains will then wash away soil that is important for farming.

A rice farm in China. The field has been flooded with water, as rice plants grow well in waterlogged soils.

Diseases

A magnified mosquito. These insects thrive in monsoon regions.

A number of serious diseases spread easily after the monsoon season, because stagnant floodwater provides an ideal breeding ground for the bacteria that cause them. Typhoid and cholera are particularly common. Mosquitoes, insects which can carry diseases such as malaria and yellow fever, also thrive in the warm, wet conditions of monsoon regions.

*Soil erosion, 115

TROPICAL DESERTS

The tropical deserts are the hottest and driest places in the world. With so little water or shelter, only a few animals and plants are able to survive in the burning heat of the day. Very few people live in tropical deserts.

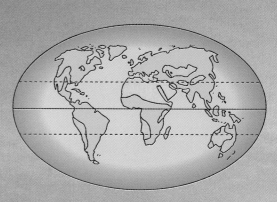

Tropical deserts exist mainly between 15° and 30° north and south of the Equator.

This is a fertile area, called an oasis, in the Thar Desert, Rajasthan, India. These people are collecting water there.

Desert climate

Most deserts are hot during the day and cold at night. During the day, the heat is intense because there are few clouds to block the Sun's rays. Temperatures can reach over 52°C (126°F). At night, the lack of clouds allows heat to escape, so temperatures can drop to below freezing.

Less than 250mm (10in) of rain falls on deserts each year. When it rains, it is usually in short, violent storms. If the land has been baked by the heat of the Sun, these brief rainstorms can cause floods because the rain is not absorbed quickly enough by the dry ground.

Oases

There is water in the desert, but most of it is stored underground in types of rocks called porous rocks*. In a few places, where these rocks are at the surface, moist areas called oases are formed. Birds, animals and people gather at oases to drink and most desert plants grow near them.

*Porous rocks, 128

Desert landscapes

Only 25% of the world's deserts are sandy. Most deserts consist of bare rock or stone. Some even have dramatic rocky mountains. In sandy deserts, sand often collects together to form hills called dunes, which move and change shape as the wind blows the sand across the desert.

Strong winds sometimes sweep across deserts, causing sandstorms which can wear away the rocks in their path. Over many years, this "sand-blasting" effect can produce some unusually-shaped rocks. The process of wearing away rocks in this way is known as erosion*.

This is a sand dune in the Sahara Desert, Africa, the biggest desert in the world. The man is one of the Tuaregs, a group of people who live in the Sahara.

Adaptation

In order to survive in the desert, those plants and animals that live there have adapted so that they are able to cope with the heat and limited supplies of water.

Some desert plants can store water in their stems or can access water deep in the ground through long tap roots. Others can reduce water loss by rolling up their leaves.

Usually animals lose lots of water in their droppings, but many desert animals have dry droppings. This helps them to save water, so that they can last longer without water.

Camels can drink gallons of water in a few minutes and then last days without any.

Desert expansion

The world's deserts are increasing in size. This process, known as desertification, is caused by the destruction of the vegetation near the edges of deserts. People living in these dry areas need grass for their animals to eat and wood from trees to burn as fuel. This destruction of vegetation means that the soil is easily washed or blown away and the water cycle* is disrupted. Once this has happened, it is very difficult for vegetation to grow there.

*Erosion, 118; water cycle, 80

MEDITERRANEAN CLIMATES

Mediterranean climates are warm temperate* climates. They get their name from the regions bordering the Mediterranean Sea. However, other parts of the world, such as small areas around Cape Town (South Africa), Perth (Australia), San Francisco (U.S.A.) and Valparaíso (Chile) also share this climate.

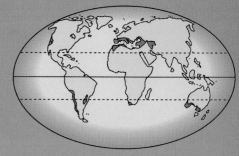

This map shows those areas with a Mediterranean climate.

Warm and dry

Mediterranean climates cover only a small part of the world. They are found on the west coasts of continents between 30° and 40° north and south of the Equator. The winters are warm and wet and the summers are hot and dry.

During the summer, warm, dry winds blow from the tropics*, bringing dry conditions. In the winter, the steady rainfall transforms the parched, brown landscape into a rich green one.

In the Mediterranean region itself, the Mediterranean Sea (an inland sea) has a crucial effect on the climate of the surrounding countries. In the summer, the sea is cooler than the land, so the air sinks down over the sea and the surrounding area. This means that there is very little rain. The lack of cloud cover also means that temperatures are high. In winter, the relative warmth of the sea causes mild winters, and warm, moist air from the sea brings rain.

In other parts of the world which have a Mediterranean climate, cold offshore currents* have a similar effect on the local climate as the Mediterranean Sea has on southern Europe.

This town in the south of France overlooks the Côte d'Azur, a stretch of coastline by the Mediterranean Sea which is a popular spot for vacations.

Oranges grow well in Mediterranean climates.

Vegetation

There are two main types of vegetation in Mediterranean regions: trees such as cork oaks and olives, and low woody plants, or scrub. The vegetation is well adapted to the dry summer climate, with thick, waxy leaves which reduce the amount of water the plant loses and long roots which enable them to reach water deep underground.

Farming

Those places with Mediterranean climates are home to some of the world's most important wine producers. Grape vines are particularly well adapted to the climate, as they have long roots and tough bark.

Tourism

People sunbathing on a beach in the Côte d'Azur, southern France

The hot, dry summers in Mediterranean countries such as Greece, Spain, Italy and southern France have made them popular vacation destinations for North Europeans from cooler climates searching for summer sunshine. This has meant that tourism has become an important part of the economy of these countries. Resorts tend to be developed in strips along the coast, where closeness to the sea and pleasant beaches are also major attractions.

A vineyard in the Douro Valley, Portugal. The grapes are being hand-picked to make wine.

The Mediterranean climate is good for growing citrus fruits, such as oranges, lemons and grapefruit. The summers are hot, which means that the fruit ripens quickly. Citrus fruits also have thick skins which help them to retain moisture so that they can survive the dry conditions.

Because Mediterranean summers are so dry, many farmers have to water the land artificially to help their crops grow. This is called irrigation.

*Ocean currents, 51; temperate, 68; tropics, 146

TEMPERATE CLIMATES

The area between the Arctic and Antarctic Circles (the Frigid Zone) and the tropics (the Torrid Zone) is called the Temperate Zone. As the term temperate suggests, temperatures are never very extreme, but this vast area contains a wide range of climates and landscapes.

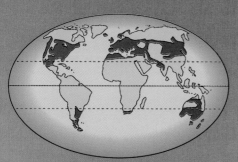

The purple areas of this map show the parts of the world with temperate climates.

Varied climates

The vegetation in the Temperate Zone ranges from forests to dry grasslands. However, all the different areas have four seasons*: spring, summer, autumn and winter. This is because of the Earth's tilt and the way that each hemisphere faces the Sun and then faces away from it.

Green lands

The mid-latitudes (between 40° and 60° north and south of the Equator) have a rainy climate, which is usually described as cool temperate. The steady rain throughout the year is the result of cool air from the poles meeting warm air from the tropics*. The warm air is forced upwards, causing swirling patterns of clouds and rain known as depressions.

The moderate temperatures in cool temperate regions mean that vegetation has a long period of uninterrupted growth, so the landscape is very green. Most trees are deciduous trees, which means that they lose their leaves in winter.

This region, which includes most of Europe, contains the richest farmland areas. The fertile soil and rainfall throughout the year make it suitable for a wide variety of crops, including grains, green vegetables and deciduous fruits.

In temperate regions, many of the trees are deciduous. This means that they lose their leaves in winter.

Before the leaves on deciduous trees fall, they change from green to orange, red and yellow.

*Seasons, 12; tropics, 146

Grasslands

A view of the huge grasslands, or prairies, of North America

The prairies of North America and the steppes of Russia are huge temperate grasslands which lie in the middle of continents. Their summers are hot and sunny, but their winters can be quite harsh because they are away from the warming effects of the ocean*.

These areas receive too little rainfall for trees to grow, so the main vegetation is grasses. In the vast, treeless prairies of North America, winter frosts break up the rich soils, but summer days are long and warm. Wheat is suited to these conditions and is grown extensively.

Seasonal life

The lives of many animals and plants in temperate regions closely follow the cycle of the seasons.

Annual plants complete their life's cycle in a year. They produce seeds which begin growing in spring and then flower in summer. In autumn, they produce seeds and fruit. At the end of the year the plants die. Perennial plants last for several years, but still produce new growth in the spring. During autumn, deciduous trees start to lose their leaves and by winter, they are bare.

In the winter, the ground often freezes, leaving few plants for animals to feed on.

Many animals prepare for the winter by storing up food. Some, such as the dormouse, cope with the lack of food by going into a deep sleep known as hibernation. During hibernation, an animal's breathing and heartbeat slow down and it does not need to eat. There are also animals that avoid the cold weather altogether by moving, or migrating, to warmer places.

A dormouse hibernating in its nest during the winter months

POLAR REGIONS

The Arctic, the area around the North Pole, and the Antarctic, the area around the South Pole, are known as the polar regions. The temperatures there are usually below freezing and huge expanses of land and sea are covered in ice and snow.

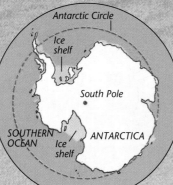

This map shows the Antarctic from above. The imaginary line around it is called the Antarctic Circle.

Antarctic

In the middle of the Antarctic Ocean is a land mass, or continent, known as Antarctica, which is covered in a thick layer of ice. Temperatures are so low that when snow falls it doesn't melt, but builds up with each snowfall. The weight of the snow on top presses down on the lower layers to form ice.

No land mammals live permanently in Antarctica because it is so cold, but some animals, such as seals, go there to breed. A number of sea birds, including penguins, live there permanently.

The emperor penguin is one of seven different species of penguin that live in the Antarctic.

This map shows the Arctic from above. The imaginary line around it is called the Arctic Circle.

Arctic

The Arctic is mainly made up of the Arctic Ocean, but its edges are bordered by several countries, including Greenland, Canada and Alaska. The land here, called the tundra, is just warm enough for animals and plants to survive.

In the summer, the ice on the tundra melts and the surface of the ground thaws. The ground often becomes boggy, because deeper down it is still frozen and the water cannot seep through. This frozen layer is called permafrost.

Keeping warm

Some polar animals have adapted to living in the sea, as icy winds make it difficult to survive on land. For example, penguins cannot fly and seals move awkwardly on land, but both are good swimmers. Other animals have adapted to cope with the cold in different ways. Polar bears have a thick layer of fat under their skin which keeps them warm. Musk oxen have thick, shaggy coats. Many polar animals have small ears, which help to reduce heat loss.

These penguins are huddling together for warmth. They take turns standing on the outside.

The Arctic fox's white winter coat means that it doesn't stand out against the snowy background.

Blending in

A number of animals in the Arctic have different winter and summer coats. As the snow falls in the winter, their coats change and become white. This enables them to camouflage themselves, or blend in with their backgrounds. During the summer a brown coat helps them to blend in more easily with the grass. Their ability to change with their environment helps these animals to hide from predators or to sneak up on their prey without being seen.

In summer, the Arctic fox's brown coat enables it to blend in with rocks and plants.

Arctic shelters

Some animals that live in the Arctic build burrows or dens in the snow to protect themselves from the cold winds. For example, polar bears build dens, with many chambers in the snow, for their cubs to take shelter.

MOUNTAINS

About 5% of the world's land surface is covered by high mountains and mountain ranges. Mountain areas have more than one type of climate because, as you go up a mountain, there are fewer particles in the air and the temperature falls.

The Great Basin Desert in Nevada, U.S.A., lies on the sheltered side, or rain shadow, of the Sierra Nevada mountains.

Mountain ranges

Most mountains are formed when the plates that make up the Earth's crust push together, forcing the land into fold mountains*. This is why mountains often occur in long lines, or ranges.

When air is blown from the sea onto a mountain range, it is forced to rise. The tiny water droplets in the air cool down, condense and turn into clouds. Rain or snow then falls on the mountainside. The sheltered land on the other side of the mountain, called the rain shadow, gets very little rain, and may become a desert.

Mountain peaks in the Andes, on the border between Chile and Argentina

Mountain levels

The higher up a mountain you go, the colder it gets. This is because the air higher up is thinner, so it can store less heat. There are different types of weather, vegetation and animal life at different heights up the mountain. Few species live on the windy peaks, but mountain goats and sheep graze on the grassy, rocky slopes below. Farther down, below a line called the treeline, it is warm enough for trees to grow. Animals such as cougars and hares live in mountain forests.

Adaptation

Mountain species are adapted to surviving in cold temperatures and strong winds. Mountain plants grow close to the ground and have deep roots, so they don't get blown away. Many mountain animals have large lungs for extracting enough oxygen from the thin air, and thick fur which keeps them warm.

The alpine forget-me-not flower is adapted to mountain climates. It has shorter, thicker stems and deeper roots than the common forget-me-not.

This shepherd from the Basque region of France is holding two baby goats. Goats are well-suited to the mountain climate.

Mountain people

Like mountain animals, people who live in high mountain areas have bigger lungs than lowlanders, to help them breathe more easily in the thin air. Mountain people may also be cut off from other cultures. For example, the Basque people, who have lived in the Pyrenees mountains between France and Spain for thousands of years, have a very unusual language which is unlike any other on Earth. This is because their mountain home meant that, for centuries, they rarely mixed with other peoples.

*Fold mountains, 19

CHANGING CLIMATES

E ver since the Earth was formed, its climate has been changing. Volcanic eruptions, collisions with asteroids, and the path of the solar system through space may all have caused climate changes that affected the atmosphere, the landscape and living things.

The red outline on this map shows the areas of the Earth that were covered in ice during the last Ice age. The white areas are those places that are still covered in ice today.

Long ago, widespread volcanic activity could have caused fires which damaged habitats, wiping out various species.

Ice ages

Throughout its history, the Earth has gone through several Ice ages, when the climate was colder than it is now, and glaciers* spread across much of the globe. Sea levels were lower as well, because a lot of the world's water was frozen into ice.

Within each Ice age, there have been slightly warmer periods called interglacials. Several thousand years ago,

the Earth was in an Ice age. Then the climate got warmer and most of the ice melted. But the Ice age may not be over. Some experts think that we are now in an interglacial period.

Ice ages have several causes. As the galaxy spins, the Earth may enter magnetic fields which shield it from the Sun's heat. It may also sometimes change its orbit, move away from the Sun and get cooler.

Explosions

Long-term climate patterns can be affected by sudden events, such as huge volcanic eruptions, or asteroids (lumps of rock from space) hitting the Earth. Events like this in the past could have filled Earth's atmosphere with smoke and dust which blocked out the sunlight, making the climate cold and dark and killing plants.

*Glaciers, 130

Geological evidence

We can tell the Earth's climate has changed by looking at rocks and fossils. Many rocks form gradually in layers. These layers provide a record of what happened, called the fossil record. In warmer periods of the Earth's history, more plants and animals were alive and more fossils were preserved. Layers with fewer fossils show colder periods, when there were fewer living things.

Landscapes also hold clues about the past. For example, a U-shaped valley shows where a glacier gouged out a channel during an Ice age.

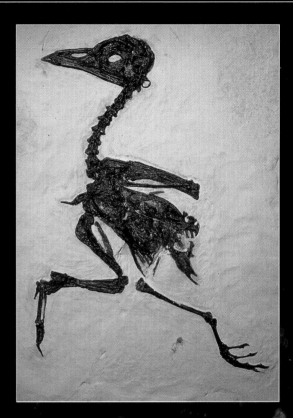

Fossils found in stone, such as this well-preserved bird fossil, can reveal which types of animals lived in which places long ago.

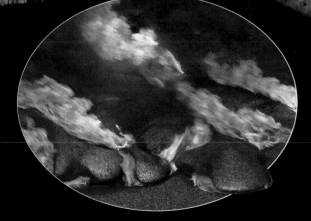

As well as blocking out vital sunlight with smoke and ash, volcanic eruptions can destroy plant life by smothering the land with lava, hot molten rock that burns everything in its path.

Moving continents

As the plates* that make up the Earth's crust have slowly changed position, the climate of each continent has altered. For example, what is now West Africa was once at the South Pole. As it got nearer the Equator, its climate warmed up as it received more sunlight. Climates are also affected by ocean currents*. As the continents separated from each other, currents could flow between them, bringing cold or warm water from other parts of the Earth.

*Glaciers, 130; ocean currents, 51; plates, 18

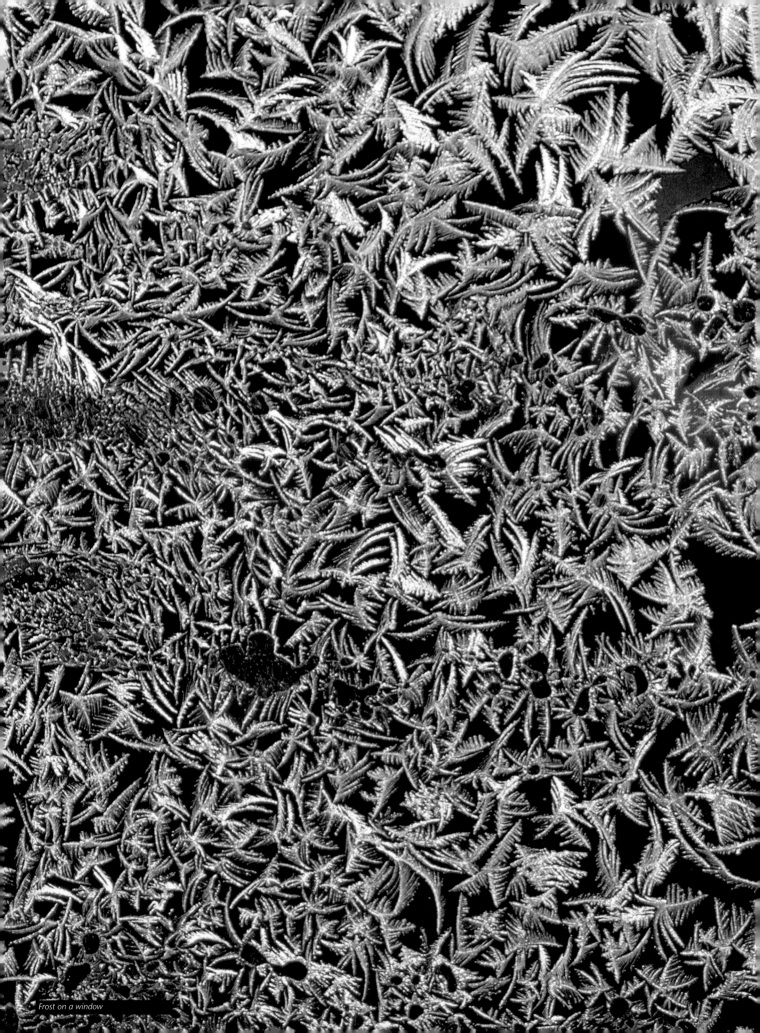
Frost on a window

WEATHER

WHAT IS WEATHER?

Weather is the way the Earth's atmosphere* behaves, whether it is hot or cold, windy or still, raining, snowing or hailing. Climate* means the overall temperature and patterns of weather in a particular place. But weather itself changes from day to day, and is much harder to predict.

The importance of weather

Weather affects everyone's life. Crops rely on the right weather conditions to grow properly. Summer vacations and trips to ski resorts may be ruined if the weather behaves unexpectedly. Weather is also a factor in many of the world's worst disasters, such as floods, landslides, ice storms, droughts and famines.

The right weather is so important that, for thousands of years, people have worshipped weather gods and used rituals to try to affect it. But, even with modern technology, it is almost impossible to control the weather.

This Japanese dancer wears a special costume and waves a large feather as part of traditional dance which is meant to make the rain fall.

*Atmosphere, 48; climate, 56; cumulus clouds, 81; evaporation, 80

What weather is

Weather is made up of three main ingredients: temperature, the movement of the air, and the amount of water in the air.

Hot weather is caused by the Sun heating up the land and the atmosphere*. If the Sun is hidden by clouds, or if a cold wind is blowing, the temperature is cooler.

Wind is also caused by the Sun. As air gets hotter, it expands, gets less dense, and rises. A mass of colder, heavier air, called a cold front, rushes in to replace it, making wind.

Finally, the Sun's heat makes water from plants, soil, rivers and seas evaporate* into the air. The water forms clouds, and may then fall as rain, snow or hail.

These three factors are always changing and affecting each other. They combine to make complicated patterns, known as weather systems. You can find out more about them on the next few pages.

The way bees behave could help us predict the weather.

Umbrellas have been used for hundreds of years to protect people from the weather. These paper umbrellas, called parasols, help to protect people from the Sun.

Traditional signs

Cumulus clouds usually appear when the weather is warm and sunny.

Today, scientists can predict the weather using satellites and computers. But before these were invented, people predicted the weather by observing signs, such as the way the clouds look, and the way animals behave. For example, cumulus clouds* usually mean sunny weather, and bees usually go home to their hives before a storm.

Weather facts

• The heaviest hailstones, weighing up to 1kg (2lb 3oz), fell in Gopalganj, Bangladesh, in 1986.

• The wettest place in the world is Tutunendo, Colombia. It gets nearly 12m (40ft) of rain a year.

• The biggest recorded snowflakes were 38cm (15in) across and fell on Fort Keogh, Montana, U.S.A., in 1887.

• The driest place in the world is Calama, Chile. Until 1971, there had been no rain there for 400 years.

WATER AND CLOUDS

The amount of water on Earth doesn't change. But water changes its state as it moves around in a huge cycle. It exists as a liquid (water) in seas and rivers, freezes into a solid (ice) which makes snow and hail, and floats in the air as clouds.

Snowflakes form when water droplets freeze into ice crystals. These snowflakes have been tinted so you can see their six-sided shapes more clearly.

The water cycle

When water is heated up, it changes from a liquid into tiny invisible water droplets that float in the air. This process is called evaporation.

The Sun's heat causes water to evaporate from rivers, lakes and seas. Plants suck up water from the ground and it escapes from their leaves as tiny droplets. People and animals breathe out water droplets in their breath.

As water droplets rise, they get cooler, because the air is cooler higher up. This makes the water condense, or turn into liquid again, to form bigger droplets which can be seen as clouds. As clouds get colder, the water droplets join together and grow bigger. When they are heavy enough they fall as rain, and flow back into rivers, lakes and seas. This process is known as the water cycle.

When water droplets in clouds become heavy, they fall as rain, snow or hail.

Water flows down to the sea in streams and rivers.

Water droplets in the air rise, cool down and form clouds.

Plants and animals take in water that has fallen as rain.

Water evaporates from rivers and seas in the heat of the Sun.

This diagram shows how the water cycle works.

Clouds

The way clouds look depends on how fast they have formed and how much water is in them. When clouds form slowly and steadily, they spread out across the sky in sheets. On hot days, clouds grow faster and puff up into heaps. Clouds full of big droplets look darker.

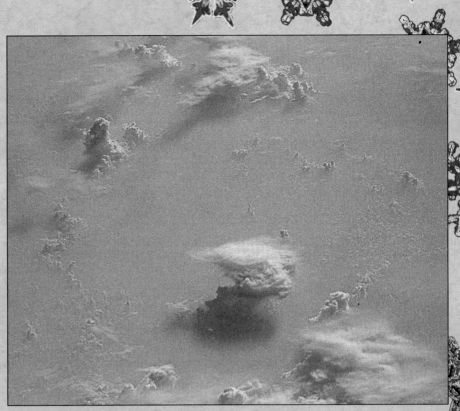

These tall, piled-up cumulonimbus clouds were photographed over the Gulf of Mexico. A cumulonimbus cloud is freezing at the top, but warmer at the bottom.

Cumulus clouds look like white, puffy heaps. They often form high in the sky in warm sunny weather.

Stratus clouds form low, flat layers and often block out the sunshine.

Cirrus clouds are high and wispy. (The word cirrus *means "like wispy hair" in Latin.)*

Precipitation

Water that falls onto the Earth's surface is called precipitation. Rain is the most common kind. There are many types of rain, from light drizzle to heavy downpours and monsoon rains*. Rain is vitally important for plants and animals, and too much or too little can be disastrous.

In freezing weather, precipitation sometimes takes the form of snow or hail instead of raindrops. The diagram on the right shows how hailstones are formed.

Hail begins as ice crystals in giant cumulonimbus clouds.

Air currents push the crystals up and around inside the cloud.

As they move, the crystals bump into water droplets, which freeze around them in layers, like the layers of an onion.

The layers of ice build up until they form heavy hailstones, which fall to Earth.

*Monsoons, 62

THUNDERSTORMS

Sometimes in warm weather, huge storm clouds form very quickly. These clouds are full of water and fast-moving air currents. They can build up a store of electricity powerful enough to make lightning and thunder.

Electric clouds

In hot, damp weather, lots of tiny invisible water droplets rise very fast. When they hit the colder air above, they make a tall, piled-up cloud called a cumulonimbus cloud.

Inside the cloud, water droplets and ice crystals rub together in the swirling air. This rubbing causes the crystals and droplets to build up a strong electric charge. Some have a negative charge (-) and some have a positive charge (+). Negative charges collect at the bottom of the cloud, making a huge energy difference between the cloud and the ground, which has a positive charge.

The difference builds up so much that it has to be equalized. A giant spark jumps between the bottom of the cloud and the ground, allowing the different charges to even out. The spark appears as a flash of lightning.

The satellite photograph on the left shows piled-up cumulonimbus storm clouds viewed from above.

Lightning zigzags through the air as it finds the easiest path from the cloud to the ground.

Ball lightning is a very rare kind of lightning which appears as a small, floating ball of bright light. It can travel through walls and has been seen inside buildings and aircraft.

Lightning

When lightning strikes, it travels first downwards, then upwards. The first stroke, called the leader stroke, is invisible. It jumps from the cloud to the ground. This creates a path for the main stroke, which sparks from the ground back up to the cloud.

The main stroke contains so much energy that it heats up the air around it. The heat makes the air expand quickly, causing an explosion. This is the loud noise of thunder.

Struck by lightning

Lightning always travels the shortest distance it can between the cloud and the ground. So it usually strikes high places, tall buildings or prominent objects such as trees or people.

Lightning quickly heats up whatever it strikes. When a tree is struck, the water in the tree boils instantly and turns into steam, which makes the trunk explode. But although lightning is dangerous, being struck is very rare. You can stay safe by avoiding trees and open spaces during storms.

WINDSTORMS

Because of the way the world spins, wind doesn't flow in straight lines, but swirls into spirals. Sometimes, wind spirals grow into terrifying storms, such as hurricanes and tornadoes, which contain the fastest wind speeds on Earth.

A satellite picture of the hurricane Typhoon Odessa

Coriolis effect

Winds are caused by high-pressure air rushing toward low-pressure areas, called cyclones. But instead of moving straight into the cyclone, the air circles around it in a spiral. This is called the Coriolis effect, and it happens because the spinning of the Earth always pushes winds to one side.

Hurricanes

Hurricanes are huge, very powerful windstorms that can be hundreds of miles wide. They only form in very warm, wet conditions, usually over the sea in tropical areas near the Equator. No one knows exactly what makes a hurricane start.

The warm, wet air has a very low pressure, so cooler winds spiral towards it.

The damp air rises higher and condenses into thick clouds. They are blown into a spiral by the wind.

After hurricanes form, they sometimes hit land and cause massive damage. Winds of up to 240km/h (150mph) destroy buildings and rip trees out of the ground. But hurricanes die down soon after they hit land, as there is not enough moisture to keep them going.

Tornadoes

Tornadoes are much smaller than hurricanes, but can be even more dangerous. Tornadoes form during violent thunderstorms, when a hot, fast-moving upward air current meets a cold, downward air current. Because of the Coriolis effect, the hot and cold currents spiral around each other into a tight funnel of clouds between the thundercloud and the ground. The wind inside a tornado's funnel can be as fast as 480km/h (300mph), the fastest wind speeds measured on Earth.

Where the funnel touches the ground, it can be up to 500m (1,640ft) wide. It roars across the land, smashing everything in its path. People, animals and even cars can be dragged into the air by its powerful winds. But tornadoes are soon over. Although hurricanes can last 10 days, most tornadoes only last a few minutes. They grow weaker and fade away as the air inside grows colder, and the pressure evens out.

A tornado looks like a huge black or grey trunk, twisting from the thunderclouds down to the ground.

Tornado Alley

Some places have frequent thunderstorms and lots of tornadoes. Part of the U.S.A., between Texas and Illinois, has so many that it is known as Tornado Alley. The worst tornado ever recorded there hit Ellington, Missouri, on March 18, 1925. It lasted 3½ hours, destroyed four towns and killed 689 people.

Sea spouts

Sometimes a tornado forms over the sea. It sucks the water up into a towering spout, reaching into the clouds above. These tornadoes are called waterspouts. Sailors used to think they were long, snake-like sea monsters.

This engraving showing monstrous waterspouts is from a 19th-century book about the weather called L'Atmosphère.

FLOODS AND DROUGHTS

Plants, animals and people need water to survive, and they rely on the weather to bring it to them. If there is too little rain, rivers dry up and crops fail. On the other hand, too much rain causes floods, which can damage crops and buildings and wash away precious soil.

Wet and dry

Some parts of the world always have more rain than others, and many places have wet and dry seasons. Rainy and dry periods like these are not usually a problem if they are regular, but too much or too little rain can be dangerous when unexpected weather changes take people by surprise.

This picture shows terrible flooding in Vietnam. People are forced to use boats to get around.

Too much rain

Normally, rainfall soaks into the ground or flows away in streams and rivers. Floods happen when there is suddenly too much water for the ground to hold, and streams, rivers and drains overflow. The extra water can come from rain, brought by heavy storms, from ice and snow on mountains melting and flowing into streams and rivers, or even from the sea spilling onto the land.

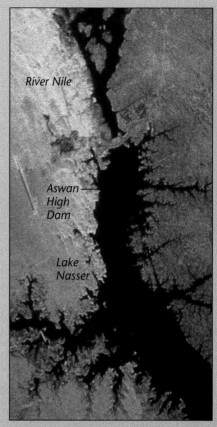

River Nile

Aswan High Dam

Lake Nasser

The River Nile floods naturally every summer, watering the land in the Nile Valley and making it fertile (good for growing crops). Lake Nasser is a reservoir formed by the Aswan High Dam.

Dirt and disease

Floods are very dangerous. As well as drowning people and animals and destroying homes and crops, floods can actually cause water shortages. They cover the land with dirty water, contaminating clean water supplies and helping diseases to spread.

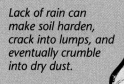

Lack of rain can make soil harden, crack into lumps, and eventually crumble into dry dust.

This pump is an important source of clean water, but the dirty floodwater surrounding it could contaminate the water supply.

Not enough rain

A drought happens when there is less than the expected amount of rain. Droughts are often hard to predict, but they usually happen when winds change direction and no rainclouds are blown over the land. A bad drought may last several years and make the land completely infertile.

The effects of droughts can be made much worse if the land has not been used carefully.

From 1931 to 1938, a severe drought hit the Southern Great Plains of the U.S.A. The farmers had overworked the land, removing the grasses that held the soil in place. As the land dried out during the drought, the soil blew away, creating violent dust storms. The area became useless for farming and was named the Dust Bowl.

FREEZING AND FRYING

These Inuit children in Alaska, U.S.A., keep warm in traditional coats called parkas, which are made from animal skins.

The temperature on Earth can range from a bone-numbing -88°C (-127°F), measured at Vostok in Antarctica, to an unbearably hot 58°C (136°F), recorded at Al' Aziziyah, Libya. Extreme hot and cold weather can be deadly, and often has strange effects on people and places.

World of ice

Ice storms are caused by rain falling onto frozen surfaces. They happen when a mass of warm air passes through a cold area in winter, bringing rain that falls in the form of liquid raindrops, instead of as snow or hail. But when the drops of water hit freezing cold roads, cars, houses and trees, they immediately freeze into a coating of solid ice.

Ice storms are beautiful, but lethal. If enough rain falls, all outdoor surfaces can get covered in a layer of ice up to 6in (15cm) thick. It makes roads hazardous to drive on, builds up on rooftops until

This branch was caught in an ice storm that hit Kingston, Canada, in 1998.

they cave in, and coats tree branches, making them so heavy that they break. The ice also weighs down power lines until they snap. With the electricity and roads cut off, people can freeze to death in their own homes.

Blizzards

Blizzards are a combination of heavy snow and strong winds. They are especially dangerous because blizzard victims are blinded by the swirling snow, as well as being caught in the freezing cold. In Yellowknife, Canada, in 1995, two soccer teams died when a blizzard hit their soccer field. The players couldn't even see far enough to find their way back to their changing rooms.

Heatwaves

A heatwave is a period of extra-hot weather. Heatwaves are caused by a combination of factors. Usually, a lack of wind and cloud allows the Sun to heat up the land and the atmosphere much more than normal. The hotter the air is, the more water it can hold in the form of tiny invisible droplets. This makes the air very humid, which makes it feel "sticky".

In some hot places, people have siestas ~ they sleep during the hottest part of the day to avoid the Sun.

This Egyptian boy's white clothes reflect the Sun's heat and help to keep him cool in hot weather.

Heatstroke

Heatstroke is caused by getting too hot ~ usually in the Sun. Normally, if you get too hot, your body sweats. The sweat evaporating from your skin helps you cool down. But heatstroke stops your body from sweating so that you get much too hot, and may go into a coma.

Heatstroke can happen quickly, especially inside a car, where the windows act like a greenhouse and stop heat from escaping. This is why animals and babies should never be left inside cars on hot, sunny days.

Sun and skin

Although the Sun provides warmth and energy, direct sunlight can be bad for you. It can cause wrinkles, sunburn and even skin cancer.

A poster warning Australians to wear t-shirts, sunscreen and sunhats

Hot and bothered

Hot, humid weather can even affect the way we behave. In New York, U.S.A., the murder rate rises as the temperature goes up. Most big riots start in cities on hot, humid nights. No one is sure why heat makes people get angry more easily.

This riot took place in the hot city of Los Angeles, in southern U.S.A., in 1992.

STRANGE WEATHER

U nusual, extreme weather, often called freak weather, can take people by surprise. Sometimes it can be so odd it doesn't seem like weather at all. Strange lights in the sky, showers of frogs, and even clouds that look like UFOs are all natural weather phenomena.

Weather beliefs

When strange weather strikes, people often think they're seeing something magical or supernatural. Weather may lie behind many traditional beliefs in fairies and ghosts, and also behind sightings of UFOs. One type of cloud, called a lenticular cloud, looks exactly like a flying saucer.

Lenticular clouds are shaped by waves of wind blowing around mountaintops. This one was seen at Mauna Kea, Hawaii, U.S.A.

Strange lights

The aurora borealis and aurora australis light up the sky around the poles with blue, red, green and white patterns. They are caused by streams of electrical particles which come from the Sun. When they interact with the gases in the Earth's atmosphere, they release energy which lights up the sky.

A solar flare is a storm on the Sun that sends electrical particles out into space, causing auroras on Earth.

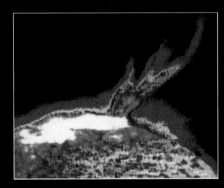

The aurora borealis appears in the northern skies, and is sometimes called the Northern Lights.

Raining frogs

"Rain" consisting of animals, fish or other objects has been reported many times through the centuries. The Roman historian Pliny reported a shower of frogs in AD77, and in the fourth century, fish fell on a town in Greece for three days. During a storm in England in 1939, so many frogs fell that witnesses were afraid to walk around in case they squashed them.

Showers like this, also known as "skyfalls", are probably caused by tornadoes* sucking up animals from ponds and rivers. Frogs are most often reported, but there have also been showers of snails, maggots, worms, pebbles and even sheep.

The common frog, a species seen falling from the sky

This magazine from May 1958 shows a skyfall of frogs which had recently been reported.

Big waves

Freak waves are one of the most dangerous types of unusual weather. Of course, not all big waves are freak waves. Hurricanes* can cause waves that swamp ships, and earthquakes can cause giant tsunami*. Some giant waves, though, appear from nowhere, even in calm weather. Scientists think waves like this may form when several smaller waves merge together.

These waves are especially dangerous because they often strike during otherwise good weather, when boats are not prepared for a storm and the crew may be out on the decks, so they can easily be swept away.

*Hurricanes, 84; tornadoes, 85; tsunamis, 44

WEATHER FORECASTING

Weather often seems random but, by careful observation, meteorologists (weather scientists) can learn how weather behaves and how to predict it. Radar and satellites help them to track clouds and watch weather patterns from space.

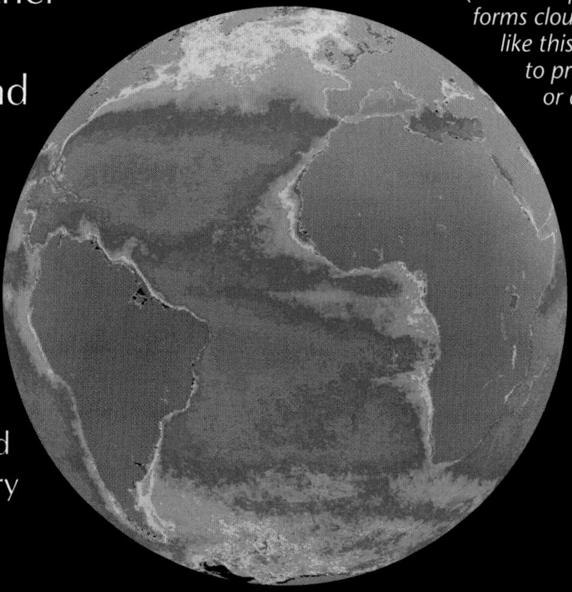

This satellite image shows the temperature of the sea. Water evaporates from warm areas (shown in pink) and forms clouds. Maps like this are used to predict rain or droughts.

Measuring weather

Meteorologists measure different aspects of the weather, such as temperature, atmospheric pressure, and the amount of rainfall, at weather stations around the world. Weather balloons and weather planes carry instruments into the sky, where they can track the movements of clouds and high-altitude winds.

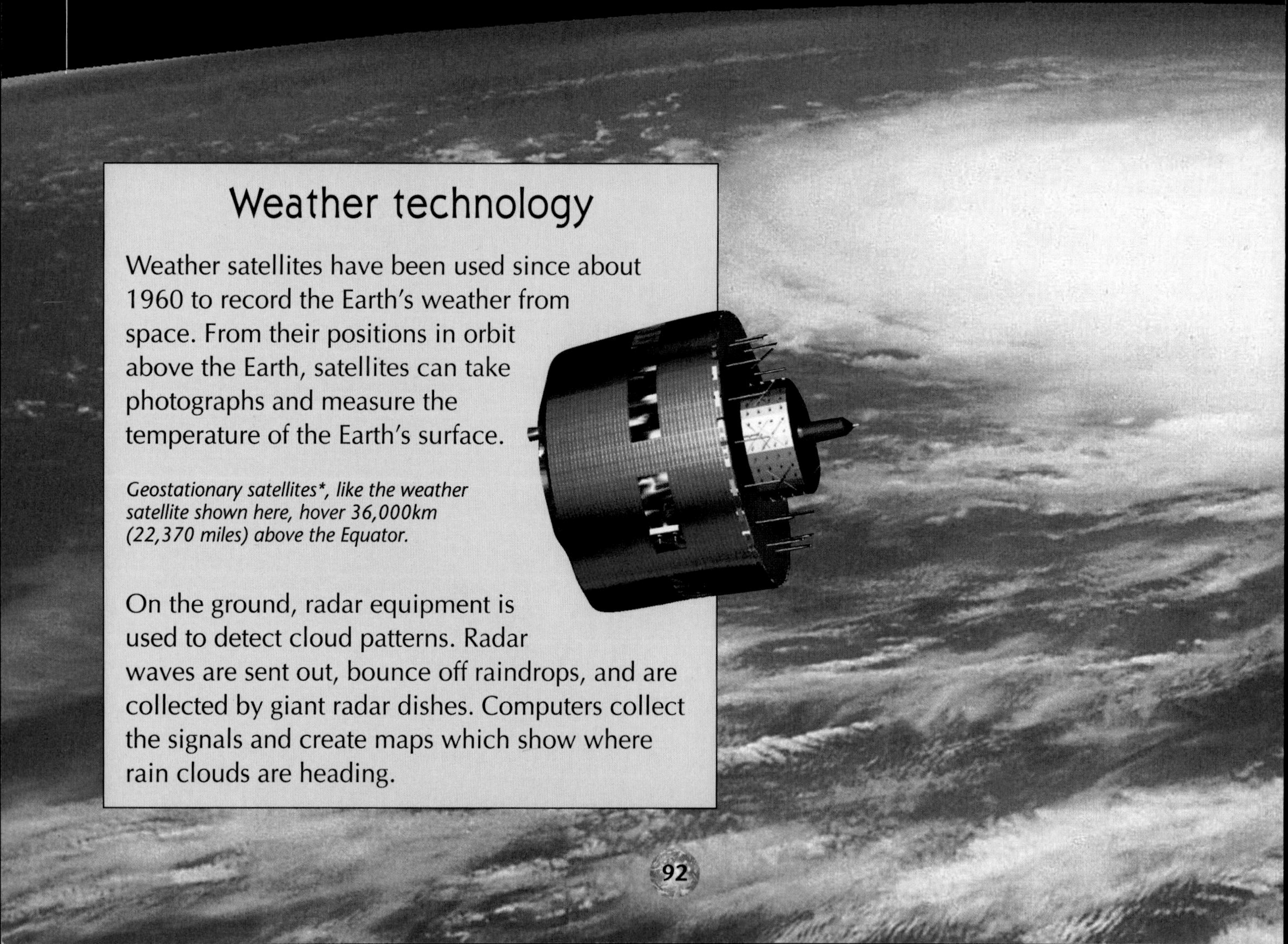

Weather technology

Weather satellites have been used since about 1960 to record the Earth's weather from space. From their positions in orbit above the Earth, satellites can take photographs and measure the temperature of the Earth's surface.

Geostationary satellites*, like the weather satellite shown here, hover 36,000km (22,370 miles) above the Equator.

On the ground, radar equipment is used to detect cloud patterns. Radar waves are sent out, bounce off raindrops, and are collected by giant radar dishes. Computers collect the signals and create maps which show where rain clouds are heading.

Predicting weather

To forecast weather, readings from weather stations and satellites are stored in powerful computers. The data can then be analysed to detect patterns and make predictions. For example, satellite images might show a hurricane forming over the ocean and heading for the coast. By calculating its size, speed, strength and direction, meteorologists can tell roughly when and where it will hit land.

At the moment, meteorologists can only predict weather a few days in advance. Weather can change so quickly that the forecasts are sometimes wrong.

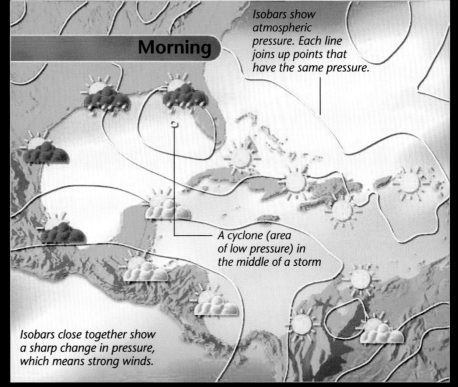

Morning

Isobars show atmospheric pressure. Each line joins up points that have the same pressure.

A cyclone (area of low pressure) in the middle of a storm

Isobars close together show a sharp change in pressure, which means strong winds.

Weather maps use lines called isobars to show changes in pressure, and symbols to indicate sunshine, rain and snow.

This picture shows a satellite photograph of a hurricane over the Pacific Ocean.

*Geostationary satellites, 11

PLANTS AND ANIMALS

A red-eyed leaf frog

PLANT LIFE ON EARTH

The Earth is the only planet so far discovered that looks green from space.

The Earth is the only planet known to support living things, or organisms. There are millions of different kinds of living things on Earth. They fall into two main groups: animals and plants. To survive, nearly all of them need light and heat from the Sun, food, water and air.

The green planet

Most plants on Earth have green leaves and stems. This is because plants contain a green substance called chlorophyll, which helps them to make their food by a process called photosynthesis. From space, the Earth's land looks mainly green. This is because of the billions of plants covering most of its surface.

Plant food

Plants feed themselves by turning light from the Sun into food chemicals in their leaves. This is called photosynthesis, which means "building with light".

For photosynthesis to happen, plants also need water and nutrients* from the soil. They absorb these through their roots. They also take in carbon dioxide, a gas found in the air, through tiny holes in their leaves called stomata. They then use all these things to make glucose, a kind of sugar which they can feed on. Oxygen and water are produced too.

The Sun provides energy, in the form of light.

A plant's flowers contain parts that make seeds. These grow into new plants.

This part of the underside of a leaf has been magnified.

Leaves convert water and carbon dioxide into glucose and oxygen.

The stalk carries water and nutrients from roots to the leaves and flower.

Leaf stalk

Stomata let carbon dioxide in, and water and oxygen out.

*Nutrients, 112

Why we need plants

Plants are essential for life on Earth. Without them, the planet would look totally different, and there would be no people or animals. Animals ~ even meat-eaters ~ need plants, because plants form the basis of all food chains*.

Plants also give out oxygen and water, which animals and people need; and their roots hold the soil together. Without them, the soil would wash away into the sea. We use plants in many other ways, such as for wood and to make medicines, fabrics and perfumes.

The aloe, one of the thousands of plants from which we extract essences, is used in cosmetics and natural medicines.

Plant babies

Like all living things, plants reproduce (make new versions of themselves). They do this by making seeds. The seeds usually form inside the flower. They may then be carried a long way by the wind before falling to the ground and beginning to grow.

A sunflower contains hundreds of seeds like these. Like the seeds of many plants, they are an important source of food for people and animals.

Types of plants

Different types of living things are called species. There are millions of species of plants, from tiny flowers to enormous trees called giant sequoias, which are the biggest living things on Earth. Different species are suited, or adapted, to living in different parts of the world. In deserts, for example, where water is scarce, cactuses grow thick stems for storing water.

A giant sequoia tree. These are found mainly in California, U.S.A.

*Food chains, 100

ANIMAL LIFE ON EARTH

There are billions of types, or species, of animals living on the Earth. They include insects, fish, birds, reptiles, amphibians, and mammals such as humans. Unlike plants, animals have to move around to find food and water.

The bald eagle is a carnivore. It feeds mainly on fish, swooping down and snatching its prey from lakes and rivers.

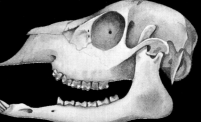

How animals live

All animals have to eat in order to survive. Herbivores eat plants and carnivores eat animals. There are some animals, such as giant pandas, that eat both plants and animals. These are called omnivores. Most humans are also omnivores.

Honeyeaters are herbivores. They feed on nectar, a sweet juice found inside flowers.

Many animals have to watch out for predators, which are other animals that want to eat them. Their bodies have to be adapted to running fast or hiding. Some animals, such as zebras, are camouflaged, which means they are patterned so that they blend in with their background and are harder for predators to see. But some predators are also camouflaged, so they can creep up on their prey.

Tools for eating

Animals' bodies are adapted to suit the kind of food they eat. Herbivores usually have flat, broad teeth designed for munching plants, while most carnivores have sharp teeth and strong jaws for grabbing and tearing up their prey (the animals they eat).

You can see the long, sharp teeth in this badger's skull. They are good for grabbing and slicing through flesh.

In this roe deer's skull, you can see the long front teeth which are suited to biting off pieces of plants and flat molar teeth which are good for chewing plants.

Natural selection

Why are animals and plants so well adapted to their way of life? One answer might be that they have gradually changed, or evolved, over a very long time to suit the places they live in and the food that is available to them.

In the 19th century, a scientist named Charles Darwin (1809-1882) put forward a theory, which he called "natural selection", to explain how these changes might happen.

According to Darwin, individual animals and plants sometimes have qualities that help them to survive. For example, in a green forest, a green bug would probably survive longer than a brown bug, because its appearance would help it to avoid being seen and eaten.

The individuals that survive the longest are likely to have more babies, and will pass on their useful qualities to them. Over a very long time, each species will very gradually develop all the most useful qualities for surviving in its own habitat.

Claws or talons

As a predator, the bald eagle has developed qualities such as good eyesight, flying skill and big strong claws, or talons. These help it to hunt and catch its prey.

Breathing

As well as eating food, animals need to breathe oxygen, a gas which is found in air and water. All animals take oxygen into their bodies, in a variety of different ways.

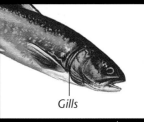

Gills

Fish have gills, which filter oxygen from the water as it flows through them.

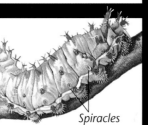

Spiracles

Insects take in oxygen through tiny holes in their bodies, called spiracles.

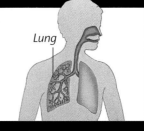

Lung

Humans and many other animals have lungs, which extract oxygen from the air.

Useful animals

Animals are very useful to humans, providing meat, milk, eggs, wool, silk, leather, and even medicines. Many animals are farmed carefully, but some species are in danger of dying out and becoming extinct, because humans have killed too many of them. You can find out more about these endangered species on page 103.

Guanacos, hunted for their long, thick wool

ECOSYSTEMS

A place where a plant or animal lives is called its habitat. For example, seas, rivers, mountains, forests and deserts are all habitats. Together, a habitat and the group, or community, of plants and animals that live in it form a whole system, called an ecosystem.

Snowy owls and lemmings are part of the ecosystem in the Arctic.

Meat-eaters survive by eating other animals found in their habitat. These cheetahs are chasing a Thomson's gazelle.

Food webs

In an ecosystem, many different food chains intertwine to make up a complicated system known as a food web. Each animal in the web may eat many different species and be hunted by several others. The diagram below shows part of a food web in a mountain forest in a northern country, such as Canada. Each blue arrow points from a species that is eaten to a species that eats it. (This is a simplified diagram. In fact, there would be many more species than this in one ecosystem, and the whole food web would be too complicated to fit on the page.)

Food chains

The animals and plants in an ecosystem depend on each other for food. One species eats another, and is in turn eaten by another. This is called a food chain. Plants form the first link in a food chain, because they make their own food from sunlight, using a process called photosynthesis*. Plant-eating animals (herbivores) eat plants, and meat-eating animals (carnivores) eat herbivores and other carnivores.

As in all ecosystems, plants form the basis of this food web.

*Photosynthesis, 96; soil, 112

Who eats who

A food web has several layers, known as trophic levels. There are different kinds of plants or animals on each level.

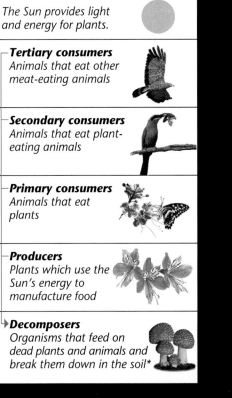

The Sun provides light and energy for plants.

Tertiary consumers
Animals that eat other meat-eating animals

Secondary consumers
Animals that eat plant-eating animals

Primary consumers
Animals that eat plants

Producers
Plants which use the Sun's energy to manufacture food

Decomposers
Organisms that feed on dead plants and animals and break them down in the soil*

The energy cycle

Plants and animals use food to make energy, which helps them grow, move, keep warm, make seeds and have babies. When plants or animals die, they are broken down by decomposers, such as fungi, and the energy goes back into the soil in the form of chemicals. These help plants to grow, and the cycle begins again.

Competition

Each type of plant or animal has a unique place in its ecosystem, known as a niche. Only one species can occupy each niche. If two different species try to exist in the same niche, they have to compete for the same food. The stronger species survives, and the other dies out or moves to a new habitat.

Different species in an ecosystem can survive side by side by eating slightly different types of food. For example, in African grasslands, elephants reach up to eat the higher branches of trees and bushes, small antelopes called gerenuks eat leaves lower down and warthogs nibble grasses on the ground. Each animal occupies a different niche, so they are not competing with each other.

Biomes

The Earth has several climate types, or biomes, such as rainforests and deserts. Each biome supports many ecosystems, but can also be seen as one big ecosystem. Together, all the biomes combine to form the biggest ecosystem of all, the Earth itself.

An elephant's long trunk allows it to reach to the tops of trees to collect food, while other animals eat the leaves lower down.

PEOPLE AND ECOSYSTEMS

Like every other plant and animal on Earth, you are part of an ecosystem. But there are now so many humans that we need more energy and make more waste than our ecosystem can deal with.

Using up energy

The first humans were suited to the ecosystems of the places they lived in. They ate the food that was available and used only as much energy as they needed to survive.

Now, though, we use up lots more energy than we really need to survive, because of all the things that modern humans do, such as running factories, getting around in cars and planes, and using electric lights and machines. We get most of our energy by burning fossil fuels*. This creates waste gases which can't be broken down quickly enough, so they build up around us as pollution.

Pollution

Pollution is any waste product that nature can't easily process and recycle. Things such as exhaust from cars, smoke from factories, and plastic packaging are all pollution.

Some pollution is just ugly, but some can be dangerous. For example, exhaust fumes that build up in the air can cause asthma, and chemicals that leak from farms into rivers can kill fish and upset the local food web*.

Smog is a kind of pollution caused when fossil fuels are burned and give off waste gases.*

Upsetting ecosystems

Each part of an ecosystem depends on all the other parts, making a natural balance. If one part is damaged or destroyed, it affects all the others.

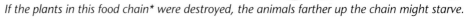

If the plants in this food chain were destroyed, the animals farther up the chain might starve.*

*Food chains, 100; food webs, 100; fossil fuels, 24

Using up space

Our farms, cities, roads and airports all need space. We use space that used to be the habitat of plants and animals. Without its habitat, an ecosystem can't work, and wild animals and plants die. If this happens too often, some species become extinct, which means they die out completely.

The dodo, which lived on the island of Mauritius, died out in about 1680 after it was hunted to extinction by Dutch settlers.

Many species have become extinct ~ for example, the dodo, a flightless bird. Extinction is sometimes caused by natural disasters such as volcanic eruptions, but usually it happens much more gradually. People now need so much space that plants and animals all over the world are dying out much faster than they used to.

Pollution, hunting, and introducing animals into new areas can cause extinctions. For example, several species of flightless birds were wiped out when humans brought dogs and cats to Australia and New Zealand.

Wind turbines like these convert the energy of the wind into electricity. This causes less pollution than burning fuel.

Conserving the Earth

Conservation means trying to reduce the damage done to the Earth and its species by pollution and other human activities. We can begin to conserve the Earth by using less energy, making less waste, and replacing as much as possible of the resources we use up. This is sometimes called sustainable living.

We cannot bring back plants and animals that are already extinct, but those that are in danger of dying out, known as endangered species, can be protected. Conservationists work to save natural habitats and protect rare wild animals from being hunted, so that they can build up their numbers and avoid extinction.

Snow leopards are an endangered species. They are now protected by laws and bred in zoos to try to save them.

POPULATION

The population of a place is the number of people who live there. The population of the world has been growing for thousands of years, and it is still growing today. There are now around 6 billion (6 thousand million) people living on Earth.

This is the city of New York in the U.S.A. It is home to 16.3 million people. Over a third of the world's population live in cities of more than 500,000 people.

Successful species

Humans are one of the most successful species on Earth. Our intelligence has allowed us to change the planet to suit our needs, and to invent technology and medicine which help us survive. Because of this, the number of people alive keeps rising.

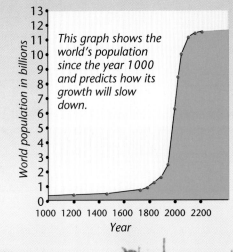

This graph shows the world's population since the year 1000 and predicts how its growth will slow down.

World population in billions

1000 1200 1400 1600 1800 2000 2200
Year

Each year, the birth rate, which means the number of people being born, is higher than the death rate. Some experts predict that the world's population could reach 10 billion by the year 2050. However, population growth is now starting to slow down. No one knows exactly what will happen, but the population of the Earth may finally stop growing during the next two hundred years.

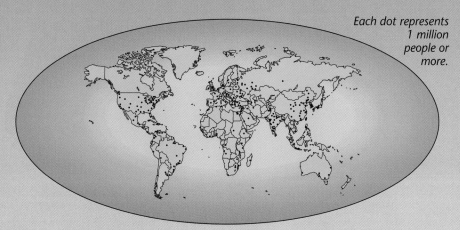

Each dot represents 1 million people or more.

This distribution map of the Earth shows at a glance the most densely populated areas and the emptiest parts of the world.

Population control

Some countries are now encouraging people to have fewer children in order to stop population growth. In China, for example, each couple is allowed to have just one child.

'put some years between us'

girl or boy two is enough

This Singaporean poster encourages couples to have no more than two children and not to have them too close together.

Overcrowding

When the population of a city grows too quickly, there may not be enough houses for people to live in, or enough jobs for people who come looking for work. This can lead to homelessness and poverty, as the city's population grows faster than the city itself.

When this happens, people with nowhere to live and very little money may be forced build their own houses out of junk and scraps. Whole makeshift towns, called shanty towns, have grown up in this way on the outskirts of big cities such as Lima in Peru, Bombay in India and São Paulo in Brazil.

This is a makeshift town, called a shanty town, on the outskirts of Cape Town in South Africa.

FARMING

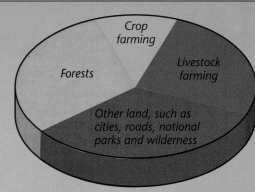

This pie chart shows how the world's land is used. Livestock farming uses more space than crop farming, but produces less food.

Most of the things you eat, a lot of what you wear, and many of the things you use come from farms. Farming means growing plants or raising animals to meet human needs. It is the biggest industry in the world.

Types of farming

Growing plants is called crop farming or arable farming, and keeping animals is called livestock farming or pastoral farming. Many farmers do a mixture of both, and this is known as mixed farming.

Farmers choose what to farm according to the type of land they have, the soil and the climate. Farms can be tiny ~ just the size of a backyard ~ or huge, like Australian sheep farms that are so big farmers use planes to travel around them.

Yaks are adapted to surviving in high mountain areas. Farmers in the Himalayas keep them for milk and wool.

Wet soil and a warm climate are ideal for growing rice. In hilly areas, farmers build steps of land, or terraces, to hold the water and soil in place. This picture shows rice terraces in China.

World industry

Around 45% of the world's workforce are farmers. Instead of just growing their own food, many farmers grow cash crops ~ crops grown specially to be sold and exported around the world. This is why, in some countries, you can buy different kinds of foods from all over the world in one supermarket.

Growing crops

Combine harvesters are used to gather all kinds of crops. This one is gathering wheat. It is much quicker than harvesting crops by hand.

Crop farming uses up around 11% of the world's land. It is the best way of producing as much food as possible from the soil, so poor countries usually grow a greater proportion of crops than rich countries do. Planting, protecting and harvesting (collecting) crops is hard work, but many farmers use machinery to do these tasks.

Animal care

Like crops, livestock has to be looked after carefully. The animals need food and water, shelter, and protection from predators and diseases. Animal products also have to be "harvested", which means collecting the animals' milk, wool or eggs, or killing them for their meat.

Farm animals often have more than one use, producing wool or skins as well as meat. In many countries they also work, pulling carts or farm machinery.

Ostriches are farmed for meat, eggs and leather, and their feathers are used in fashion accessories.

FARMING METHODS

Farmers want to get as much as they can from their land. There are various ways of improving the yield, or the amount of food or other things produced on a piece of land, but there can be problems as well.

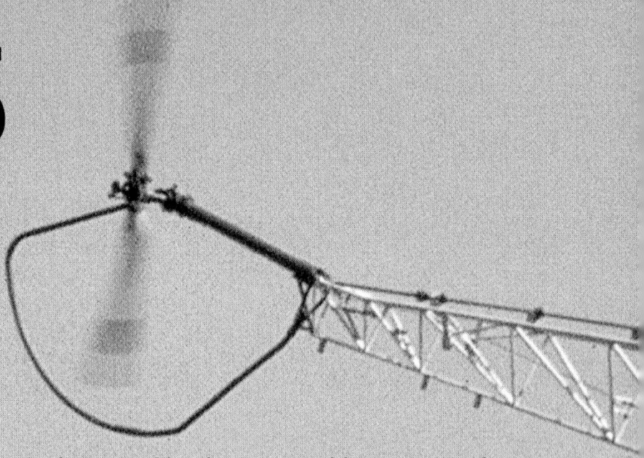

Helicopters like this are used by intensive farmers to spray fertilizers or pesticides onto their crops.

Choosing the best

An important part of farming is selective breeding, which involves choosing the best plants and animals and developing them to make more useful varieties. For instance, wheat started off as a type of grass called einkorn, which grows naturally. Early farmers chose the einkorn with the biggest seeds for replanting, because these would provide more food. Gradually, einkorn developed into modern wheat, which has lots of large seeds on each stalk. Animals are developed in the same way, by selecting and breeding those with the most useful qualities.

Modern farmed wheat

A grass called einkorn, which was developed into modern wheat

Modern farm pigs, such as Landrace pigs (right), are descended from wild boar (below).

Some of the chemical spray used by farmers may be carried by the wind and affect other areas.

Intensive farming

Intensive farming means using chemicals and technology to get as much as possible out of the land. Intensively farmed animals, such as pigs or hens, are kept in small stalls or cages to save space. They are fed by automatic water and food dispensers and may be given drugs to make them grow faster. Intensive farming can increase yields, but the chemicals used can also cause pollution.

Chemical spray units attached to a helicopter

Organic farming

Organic farming means farming without using artificial chemicals or processes. Organic farmers use animal dung or compost instead of artificial fertilizer, and don't give animals drugs to make them grow faster. Organic food is expensive, because without drugs and artificial chemicals, diseases are harder to control and yields fall. However, there is a demand for organic products from people who are worried about their health, pollution and animal welfare.

Some people think intensive farming is cruel, because the animals are kept in unnatural conditions. "Free range" animals live in more natural conditions and are allowed to move around, or range freely.

Bug warfare

Insects and other bugs that eat farm crops can be a big problem. Intensive farmers (see right) often spray crops to kill insects, but organic farmers do not use chemical sprays. Instead, they sometimes try biological pest control. They change the ecosystem* in their fields by introducing another species to feed on the pest species.

These tiny aphids damage many crops. Instead of spraying, some farmers release other insects to eat the aphids.

Intensively farmed battery hens live in small cages and are usually fed by machines. The eggs they lay roll into a tray and are carried away on a conveyor belt.

*Ecosystems, 100

Pebbles on a beach in Oregon, U.S.A.

SHAPING THE LAND

SOIL

Soil covers most of the Earth's land surface. It is made up of particles of rocks and minerals, dead plant and animal matter, tiny living organisms, gases and water. Soil is vital to life on Earth, because it provides the food and conditions plants need to grow.

As they burrow through the soil, earthworms drag dead leaves and other organic matter down to the lower levels, and break them down into humus.

What's in the soil?

The particles of rocks and minerals that are found in soil have broken away from larger rocks. They range from big chunks of stone to tiny mineral particles which get dissolved by the water in the soil. Some minerals are taken in by plants and used as food. These are called nutrients.

Soil also contains organic matter ~ dead plants and animals. When they die they are gradually broken down into a substance called humus, by all the tiny creatures, bacteria and fungi in the soil. Humus is what makes soil rich and fertile (easy for plants to grow in).

Living things, such as bacteria and fungi, are a vital part of the soil. If they weren't there to break down dead plants and animals, the remains of things that have died would keep piling up on the Earth's surface.

Soil also contains spaces filled with water and gases. Water soaks into the ground from rain, and gases come from the air and from plants and animals. Plants absorb water and gases

This earwig and her babies are among the thousands of insects and other small animals that live in soil.

Soil layers

If you looked at a slice of soil under the ground, you would see that it has several different layers, called horizons.

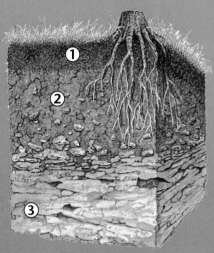

① *The topsoil contains a lot of humus and is full of tiny living creatures.*

② *Subsoil is made up of humus, rocks and minerals. Cracks and holes, or pores, in the subsoil help water to drain away, preventing the soil from getting too wet.*

③ *Bedrock is the lowest layer, or the rock that lies underneath the soil. Chunks of it sometimes break off into the soil.*

Types of soil

There are thousands and thousands of different types of soil. Some are more fertile than others, but different plants prefer different soils. So farmers can choose what to grow, depending on the type of soil they have on their land.

There are three main soil textures ~ sand, silt and clay. Sandy soil is rough and grainy. Silt has small particles, which are hard to see, while clay soil is made of fine particles, which bind together with water to form a thick, creamy mud. Clay is used to make pottery and china.

This picture shows parsnip roots reaching into the soil for water and minerals. Parsnips grow well in sandy and clay soils.

This hand contains sandy soil. Its grainy texture allows moisture to drain through it easily.

A handful of fertile soil contains up to 6 billion bacteria.

This hand contains loam soil. It is a very fertile soil containing a mixture of clay and sandy soils.

LOOKING AFTER SOIL

Why do we need to look after soil? The answer is that pollution, farming and cutting down trees can all damage soil and upset its natural balance. If we want to keep using the soil to grow food, we have to protect it, and replace all the chemicals that farming takes away.

This farmer in Minnesota, U.S.A., is loading up manure to spread over his land as a fertilizer.

The soil cycle

Where there is no farming, soil is part of a continuous cycle. Minerals are gradually dissolved into the soil. Dead plants and animals fall onto the ground, begin to rot, and are broken down into humus*. The minerals and the humus provide nutrients (food) for new plants, and the cycle starts again. This means that the nutrients that are taken out of the soil eventually get put back in.

But, when soil is used for farming, the crops are taken away to be sold, instead of rotting back into the ground. This causes the soil to become gradually less fertile* as it loses its nutrients.

Fertilizing

The best way to replace the nutrients in soil is to add a fertilizer. Fertilizers contain chemicals, such as nitrates, which plants need in order to grow. Manure (animal dung) is a natural fertilizer, but many farmers use specially made chemical fertilizers. Sometimes, if farmers use too much fertilizer, the chemicals can leak out of the soil into rivers, causing pollution.

Crop rotation

Crop rotation means changing the crop grown on a piece of land each year. It helps to keep the soil fertile, especially if the land is sometimes left to "lie fallow". This means the farmer doesn't harvest the crop, but lets it rot back into the soil. Plants such as legumes (peas and beans) or clover make good fallow crops because they put nitrates into the soil instead of taking them out.

Bright yellow oilseed rape is used to make cooking oil and as food for animals. Oilseed rape crops are often rotated with other crops on farms in Europe.

*Fertile, 112; humus, 112; terraces, 106

Soil erosion

In the natural environment, plants and trees hold soil together and stop it from being washed away by the rain or blown away by the wind. But farmers have to dig up the land to plant crops. This leaves the bare soil exposed to the wind and rain, so it is in danger of being blown or washed away.

This can also happen if trees are chopped down for firewood or to clear space for farming, especially on hillsides. Without the trees to protect it, the soil is soon washed away. This has resulted in whole forests disappearing. However, there are some ways to protect the soil.

With the trees cut down, the soil on this hillside could soon be washed away.

This cover crop protects the soil between rows of rubber trees. It also lets farmers grow two crops on the same land.

In some places, farmers can grow crops among the trees without cutting them down. If a crop leaves bare patches of soil, a crop called a cover crop can be planted in the gaps to stop it from eroding. In hilly areas, farmers build walls called terraces* to hold soil in place.

Lost forever

Ancient ruins show that there were once busy towns in places that are now desert, such as parts of Egypt and Saudi Arabia.

7,000-year-old pottery jars from an ancient civilization called Mesopotamia. The area where they were found is now desert.

The people who lived there may not have known how to look after soil and stop it from eroding. This may be why their civilizations died out.

WEATHERING

The rocks that make up the Earth's surface are constantly being worn away and broken down by the weather and by the actions of plants and animals. This process is called weathering.

How weathering happens

There are two main ways weathering can happen. Chemical weathering happens when chemicals, such as acid, in rainwater, gradually dissolve and eat away at rocks. Physical weathering makes rocks break apart in sheets, blocks or grains. It is usually caused by extremes of hot and cold.

Dissolving rock

Chemical weathering is usually caused by rainwater. The water absorbs gases from the air and the soil, making a weak acid. The acid eats away at certain types of rocks, creating cracks and holes which then let in more water and grow bigger.

The holes in this limestone on Kangaroo Island, Australia, were caused by acid, in rainwater, eating away at it.

Breaking apart

Heat makes most substances grow, or expand, very slightly. When rocks are warmed by the Sun, they expand, and when they cool down at night they shrink, or contract. The outer layer of the rock expands more, because it is directly exposed to the Sun's heat. Eventually it separates from the rock and peels off. This is called exfoliation.

Another type of weathering, freeze-thaw action, is caused when water seeps into cracks in rock and then freezes and expands.

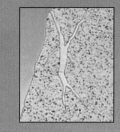 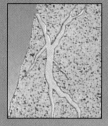 

The process of freeze-thaw action begins when rain seeps into a small crack in a rock.

The water freezes, expands and widens the crack. When the ice thaws, more water can seep in.

As the temperature rises and falls, the crack gradually grows until the rock breaks apart.

Biological weathering

Weathering caused by plants or animals is called biological weathering. For example, lichens, which are organisms that grow on rocks, give out acidic chemicals which eat away at the rock surface. Animals burrowing and roots growing in the ground can also contribute to rocks breaking down.

As well as being dissolved by acidic rainwater, the Kangaroo Island rock on the left is being eaten away by lichens ~ the red areas on its surface.

Shaping the landscape

Because some rocks are harder and more resistant to weathering than others, they wear away at different rates. Harder rocks get left behind as outcrops, which stick up out of the surrounding land, or as long ridges. Over many years, weathering can produce amazing rock shapes, jutting mountain peaks and deep limestone caves*.

This cave is still being shaped by chemical weathering, as acidic water eats away at cracks in the rock.

*Limestone caves, 129

EROSION

You can sometimes tell old mountains from younger ones by how worn and flattened they are.

E rosion happens when wind, water and gravity carry away particles of rocks and soil that have been worn down by weathering*. Gradually, eroded material is carried downhill and into rivers, and most of it ends up being washed into the sea.

K2 in the Himalayas is 8,611m (28,250 ft) high. It is relatively young and still has pointed peaks.

Mount Baker in Washington, U.S.A. is 3,285m (10,778 ft) high. It has a flatter, worn shape, showing it was formed earlier in the Earth's history.

Wind and rain

Over hundreds of years, wind gradually blows away tiny particles from the surface of rocks. Many rocks contain different minerals, some harder than others. The wind wears them away at different rates, carving the rock into wind sculptures.

Rain splashing onto rocks and soil washes away bigger particles and carries them into rivers. Farmers have to protect the soil* to prevent it all from eroding away in the rain.

These pinnacles in Arizona are striated, which means the wind has carved their surface into narrow grooves.

Moving mountains

On mountains, particles of rocks and soil are pulled downhill by gravity. Chunks of rock that break off near the top of a mountain fall down the slopes, knocking off other chunks as they go. Often a covering of loose stones, called scree, collects at the bottom of a slope.

Humans can add to this kind of erosion. Rock climbers sometimes dislodge scree and set off rockfalls, and walkers can slowly wear mountain paths away.

Wearing flat

As erosion carries particles of rocks and soil away from mountains and high ground towards the sea, the Earth's land masses become lower and smoother. However, new islands and mountains are sometimes formed by volcanoes* erupting and by the plates* that make up the Earth's crust grinding together. So as old land is worn away, new land rises up to replace it.

This photo shows the bare hillside left behind after a landslide in North Carolina, U.S.A.

Landslides

A landslide is a mass of earth and rock suddenly slipping down a steep slope. One of the worst happened in 1903, when over 30 million m³ (40 million cubic yards) of rock fell down Turtle Mountain in Canada, and landed on the town of Frank, killing 70 people. This landslide, like most landslides, was caused by rainwater soaking into the soil and making it heavier. Landslides are particularly likely if water soaks into a layer of shale (a type of slippery rock made from compressed clay). The rocks, soil and trees on top may all slip down the mountainside.

Preventing erosion

A certain amount of erosion is normal, and we could never stop it completely. In some places, though, we can try to slow it down.

On mountains that are popular with walkers, stone or wooden paths help to protect the land from being worn away by feet. In hilly areas, trees help to keep the soil in place and prevent landslides, so people have learned not to cut down hillside trees.

A worker planting vegetation to prevent erosion near a roadside

Plates, 18; soil erosion, 115; volcanoes, 28; weathering, 116

A group of Atlantic salmon swimming

RIVERS AND OCEANS

RIVERS

The water in rivers comes from rainfall, from snow and ice melting from mountains and glaciers, and also from water inside the Earth, called groundwater. Rivers carry all this water downhill and into lakes and oceans.

Hippopotamuses live in and around slow, muddy rivers in Africa. This hippopotamus is providing a resting place for an egret.

A river's course

A river changes as it flows downhill along its path, or course. Many rivers begin in mountain areas, where rain and melting ice run into steep, clear streams. The water is rough, so the plants and animals that live in it have to be able to cling onto the rocks or swim against the stream to avoid being swept away.

As mountain streams reach the valleys, they begin to join together. Smaller streams and rivers that flow into a bigger, broader river are called tributaries. Away from the mountains, the water is warmer and flows more smoothly, so different plants and animals are found. As the land levels out, the river starts to meander, or twist from side to side, forming large loops and bends.

Finally, the river widens out into a broad estuary, or sometimes splits into a network of channels called a delta*, before flowing into the sea (or sometimes into a large lake). The part of a river where it meets the sea is called the river mouth.

Mountain streams, like this one in Connecticut, U.S.A., form series of mini waterfalls as they tumble down over the steep, rocky slopes.

Drainage

The area of land from which a river collects water is called its drainage basin. When water drains into streams and rivers, it forms different patterns, depending on the shape of the land and the type of rocks it is made of.

When there is only one type of rock, streams form a tree-like pattern like this. It is called a dendritic drainage pattern.

River records

The Manú River, a tributary of the Amazon, winding its way through the rainforests of Peru

The longest river in the world is the River Nile in Africa. It travels northward for over 6,600km (4,100 miles) from its source in Burundi to its delta in Egypt, where it flows into the Mediterranean Sea. But, the world's biggest river, or the one that holds the most water, is the Amazon in South America. It is about 6,440km (4,000 miles) long, and flows across South America from west to east. Every single second, it pours about 94 million litres (20 million gallons) of water into the Atlantic Ocean. At its mouth, the Amazon is 240km (150 miles) wide.

A Nile crocodile stalks its prey by swimming silently along in the river, with most of its body underwater.

*Deltas, 124

RIVER EROSION

Rivers can carve through solid rock and move huge boulders hundreds of miles. Over many years, rivers have eroded deep gorges and huge waterfalls, and carried vast amounts of rock, sand, soil and mud to the sea.

This satellite photo shows the Mahakam River, in Borneo. You can see how a network of channels and islands, or a delta, is formed where the river runs into the sea.

How rivers erode

As a river flows, the water sweeps along any loose soil, sand or rocks in its way. As they roll, slide and bounce along, the rocks and pebbles chip away at the riverbed, making it deeper and wider. They also grind against each other, which wears them down and breaks them into smaller pieces.

The river also forces water and air bubbles into cracks in the riverbed, breaking off more chunks of rock and soil. Another reason rivers erode is that river water is slightly acidic, because it comes from rain*. It gradually wears away some types of rocks by dissolving them.

These rocks have been smoothed and rounded by the action of the water in the river.

Deposition

As a river flows over flatter land and slows down, it starts to drop, or deposit, some of the rocks and particles it is carrying. The biggest rocks are deposited first. Then, as the river gets slower, it starts to deposit sediment, made up of sand, soil and mud. This is why slow, wide rivers have muddy riverbeds. Near the sea, the sediment may form whole islands. The river splits up and forms a network of channels called a delta. The rest of the sediment flows into the sea and onto the seabed.

*Meander, 122; rainwater, 116

Changing course

Rivers flow faster around the outside of a bend, or meander*, than on the inside. The outside edge is gradually eroded, while the river deposits debris on the inside edge. This means that the meander grows longer and narrower over time. Eventually the two sides of the meander meet each other, and the river cuts through to form a new, straighter course. The entrance to the meander gradually fills up with sediment, leaving a lake called an oxbow lake, or billabong.

A river erodes the outside of a bend and deposits sediment on the inside, making a loop.

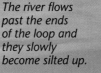

The loop grows longer and narrower until the river finally breaks through.

The river flows past the ends of the loop and they slowly become silted up.

Eventually the loop gets cut off completely and forms a lake called an oxbow lake.

This is the Horseshoe Falls, part of Niagara Falls, which is a huge waterfall on the border between Canada and the U.S.A. The waterfall moves upstream by around 3m (11ft) per year.

Waterfalls

Waterfalls begin when a river flows from an area of hard rock onto soft rock. The river wears away the soft rock more quickly and forms a ledge. Water falling over the ledge erodes a hollow at the bottom called a plunge pool. The action of the water and pebbles churning in the plunge pool can undercut the hard rock, creating an overhanging ledge. Chunks of the overhanging rock break off and very gradually, over hundreds of years, the waterfall moves backward, cutting a deep valley called a gorge.

This diagram shows how a waterfall is formed.

Waterfall cutting back

Falling water cuts away at the soft rock below.

Hard rock

Plunge pool

Softer rock

Spray undercuts here.

USING RIVERS

Rivers are central to the way human civilization has developed. They have been used for thousands of years for drinking and washing and as transport routes. Farming and industry depend on the water they provide and we can convert their flowing force into useful energy.

This engraving shows London, England, in 1631, with large ships plying their trade up and down the River Thames.

Amsterdam in the Netherlands is not on the sea, but is an important port, with over 80km (50 miles) of canals dividing it into over 80 islands.

River ports

A port is a city where ships can load and unload. When most international transport was by sea, many large ports, such as Montreal in Canada, Manaus in Brazil, and London in England, grew up near navigable rivers, that is rivers that can be used by ships. For example, most of the Amazon is navigable, because it is so wide and deep.

Canals

Canals are artificial waterways built to replace or extend rivers. Irrigation canals, for instance, divert water from rivers onto farmland. Navigational canals are built for boats or ships to travel on. For example, the Suez Canal joins the Mediterranean Sea to the Red Sea, so that ships can take a short-cut from Europe to the Indian Ocean.

Unlike natural rivers, canals do not change their course over time. They suffer less erosion* than natural rivers, because their beds and banks are usually built of brick or concrete, which wears down more slowly than natural rock and soil. Sometimes, especially in cities, natural riverbanks are rebuilt in the same way to prevent them from eroding.

*River erosion, 124

Clean energy

Electrical energy from waterpower is called hydroelectric power or HEP. An HEP plant usually consists of a dam built on a river to create a large reservoir or lake. High-pressure jets of water are released from the lake through narrow channels, and used to spin turbines which produce electricity.

Waterpower is increasingly important as an energy source. Unlike fossil fuels, it is renewable (it won't run out). It also causes very little pollution. But there can be problems when hydroelectric reservoirs take up precious land, or dams collapse.

Part of the Shasta hydroelectric dam in California, U.S.A. The spillway in the picture releases water to stop the dam from overflowing.

Dam disasters

The present-day ruins of the Malpasset Dam in France, which burst in 1959.

In the past, several large dams have caused disaster by breaking or overflowing. One example is the Malpasset Dam in Fréjus, France. It collapsed in 1959, causing a flood which killed over 500 people. The dam failed because it was built on a rock called schist, which cracks easily.

This small waterwheel generates electricity for a rural area of Washington State, U.S.A.

Waterpower

The energy in a river can be converted into electricity or other useful forms of energy. The earliest waterpower systems used a river or stream to turn a waterwheel. The turning force of the wheel was then used to drive machines, such as mills for grinding flour. Simple waterwheels like this are still used in many countries.

WATER IN THE GROUND

Water doesn't just flow over the surface of the Earth; it flows under it too. As well as the rivers and lakes that we can see, there is a huge amount of water, called groundwater, stored underground in rocks and caves.

Bottling mineral water and spring water to sell as drinking water is a major industry in some areas.

Groundwater

Many types of rocks are porous, which means they can soak up and hold water like a sponge. Groundwater is rainwater that has soaked down through the soil and then been soaked up, or absorbed, into a layer of porous rock, such as sandstone, under the ground.

Groundwater seeps through the rock until it meets a layer of impermeable rock, which won't let water pass through it. The porous rock gets filled up with water. The top level of this water is known as the water table.

Aquifers are layers of porous rock that can hold water. Some stretch for thousands of miles under the ground. In some places they are an important source of fresh water.

Springs

A spring is a stream of fresh water springing out of the ground. Springs form where a layer of water-filled porous rock meets the surface of the Earth, especially on a hillside. The groundwater flows out of the rock and forms a small pool or stream.

Spring water is often clean and sparkling because it has been filtered through layers of rock. Sometimes the water dissolves minerals from the rocks. Some of these minerals are thought to be good for your health.

Rain and snow seep through porous rock.

Water table

Saturated rock

Aquifer (porous rock)

Mountain rivers

Rivers, lakes and springs may appear where an aquifer meets the surface.

A spring emerges where saturated rock meets the surface.

Lake

Impermeable rock

Rivers under the ground

As well as soaking through rock, water can be found in underground rivers, waterfalls and even large lakes in caves and tunnels. These usually form in limestone, a type of rock that is easily dissolved by water. As water soaks into cracks in the limestone, it eats away at the rock by the process of chemical weathering* and eventually hollows out huge underground caverns and channels.

Stalactites and stalagmites

In some caves, long columns of stone, called stalactites, hang from the ceiling, and columns called stalagmites rise up from the floor. They are formed when water full of dissolved minerals drips from the cave roof. With each drop, a tiny deposit of rock is left behind. Over time, the deposit grows into a long pole. As the drips hit the cave floor, they deposit more minerals, which build up into stalagmites.

These stalactites are constantly growing as more water drips off them, depositing a tiny amount of dissolved rock with each drip.

Inside this cave in Mexico, long stalactites have grown down from the ceiling, while water has gathered to form a still underground pool.

*Chemical weathering, 116

RIVERS OF ICE

A glacier is a huge mass of ice that flows downhill, a little like a river. Glaciers flow much more slowly than rivers. But, because they are solid, they cut through the landscape more easily, gouging deep U-shaped valleys as they sweep rocks and soil along with them.

This is a glacier in Glacier Bay National Park, Alaska, U.S.A.

Ice force

Glaciers are very heavy and powerful. As a glacier flows along, the ice and the rocks caught in it scrape soil and rock from the sides and floor of the valley, carving a deep channel. When the ice melts, it deposits thick layers of debris, called moraine, on the valley floor. Glaciers also pick up boulders and deposit them further down the valley. These boulders are known as erratics.

How glaciers form

Glaciers are found in cold places, such as high mountains. At the top of a glacier, known as the accumulation zone, layers of snow collect and become packed down into hard, solid ice. As more snow falls on top, the mass of ice gets heavier and heavier, until it starts to move down the mountain.

As the ice gradually flows downhill, it gets warmer, because the air is warmer lower down*. At the lower end, called the ablation zone, the glacier melts and the icy-cold water, which is known as meltwater, flows into streams and rivers.

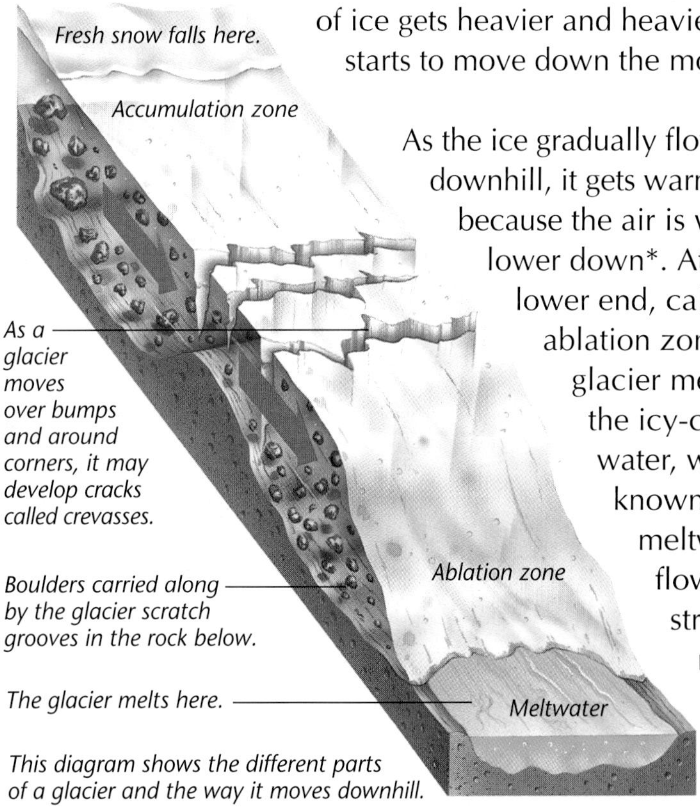

Fresh snow falls here.

Accumulation zone

As a glacier moves over bumps and around corners, it may develop cracks called crevasses.

Boulders carried along by the glacier scratch grooves in the rock below.

Ablation zone

The glacier melts here.

Meltwater

This diagram shows the different parts of a glacier and the way it moves downhill.

Glacial clues

If the climate gets warmer, glaciers sometimes melt, leaving behind a glacial valley. You can recognize a glacial valley by its deep, rounded U-shape and by debris, such as boulders and moraine hills, or drumlins, left on the valley floor. Sometimes, valleys called hanging valleys, that once joined the glacier, are left high above the main valley.

At the coast, some glacial valleys are filled in with seawater. They form narrow inlets called fjords.

This diagram shows some of the features that will help you to recognize a glacial valley. A glacial valley filled with seawater, like this, is called a fjord.

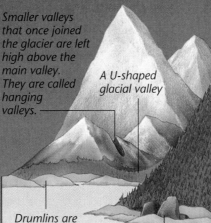

Smaller valleys that once joined the glacier are left high above the main valley. They are called hanging valleys.

A U-shaped glacial valley

Drumlins are low rounded hills, probably formed by deposited debris.

Boulders known as erratics are sometimes deposited by glaciers.

Ice sheets

Not all glaciers are found on mountains. They also form in very cold places near the poles, such as Greenland and Antarctica. Here, ice collects in huge sheets, called continental ice sheets. They flow outwards at the edges, as more snow falls, and more ice forms in the middle. Parts of the glacier can be pushed right into the sea and break off, forming icebergs.

Icebergs float away into the ocean, gradually melting as they reach warmer areas.

131

THE EDGE OF THE SEA

The coast, where the land meets the sea, is constantly being broken down and built up by the action of waves. The ebb and flow of the tide means that the environment at the seashore is always changing. Specially adapted animals and plants make their homes there.

Waves

Waves form far out at sea and are blown across the ocean by the wind. Although waves travel through water, they do not move the water itself forward. Instead, they make water particles move in circles under the surface. When a wave reaches shallow water, these circles are interrupted and the wave breaks.

Out at sea, wind blows the surface of the ocean into waves.

The waves make particles of water move in circular patterns under the surface.

On a shallow, flat beach, waves break before they reach the shore.

On a sloping coast, waves break at the shore and crash onto the beach.

On a very steep slope, waves do not break, but surge against the shore.

Coastal erosion

This archway in Dorset, England, is called Durdle Door. It was created over many years by the destructive action of waves. It started as a headland with caves on either side. The waves gradually eroded the caves until, eventually, they broke through, creating an arch.

Waves that crash onto the shore are known as destructive waves, because they gradually wear away, or erode, the coast. When they break onto beaches, they drag sand, pebbles and other debris out to sea. When they crash onto rocky cliffs, any debris they are carrying is flung against the rock, wearing it down. Waves force water and air into cracks in cliffs, carving out caves.

Destructive waves erode the coastline at different rates. Soft rock wears down quite fast, and is worn away into curved bays. Hard rock is left behind, forming cliffs and jutting pieces of land called headlands. Sometimes two caves form on either side of a headland, and the sea breaks through, leaving an arch. The arch may collapse, leaving a tower of rock called a stack.

*Tides, 149

Building beaches

While destructive waves wear away parts of the coast, other waves, called constructive waves, wash up debris onto the shore, forming beaches. When a wave breaks gently onto a flat coast, it slows down and loses energy. This makes it drop any debris it may be carrying, such as pebbles and grains of sand previously broken off into the sea from cliffs and rocky shores. Over time, this deposited material builds up into a beach.

Stones and pebbles in the sea are polished and rounded by the action of the waves.

Tides

Tides* are caused by the gravity, or pulling force, of the Moon. The Moon pulls the sea slightly towards it. So, as the Earth spins, the part nearest the Moon has a high tide. There are roughly two high tides each day.

Animals and plants that live on the seashore have to be able to survive in the water at high tide, and in the air at low tide. They also have to find ways to avoid being smashed to pieces or swept away by crashing waves.

Crabs, like this rock crab, can breathe in both water and air. They have hard shells to protect them from the sea, and can burrow into the sand to hide from predators.

Coastlines

Over many years, the action of the sea changes the shapes of countries, as it builds up the land in some places and wears it away in others. Buildings near the sea sometimes fall in or get washed away as the land is gradually eroded.

For example, the coast of Holderness in Lincolnshire, England, has worn away very quickly. Over 50 coastal villages, which were listed in a national survey of towns and villages called the Domesday Book in 1086, have been washed away into the sea.

SEAS AND OCEANS

More than two thirds of the Earth's surface is covered with salt water. The Earth's five oceans and all its seas are connected, so sea water flows freely between them. The seas and oceans, and the creatures that live in them, still hold many mysteries for scientists to explore.

The ballan wrasse fish is found mainly near rocky shores in Europe.

Under the sea

Near the land, the seabed slopes gradually downhill, forming a wide shelf called the continental shelf. At the edge of the shelf, a cliff called the continental slope drops away to the deeper part of the ocean floor, which is called the abyssal plain.

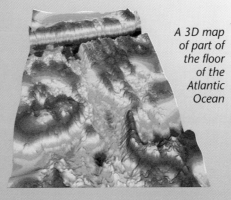

A 3D map of part of the floor of the Atlantic Ocean

Just like the land, the abyssal plain has valleys, hills, mountains and even volcanoes. It also has ridges* where new rock is pushed out from inside the Earth, and trenches* where the Earth's crust is swallowed up again.

Exploring the sea

Sea scientists, called oceanographers, find out about how the Earth was formed and how life began, by studying the seabed and the creatures that live there. Oceanographers visit the seabed in mini-submarines called submersibles, or explore it from the surface using unmanned robots called Remote Operated Vehicles (ROVs). They also map the seabed using sonar. This sends out sounds which are reflected back as echoes, showing how deep the seabed is.

*Food chains, 100; ridges, 18; trenches, 18

Life in the oceans

Seas and oceans contain a huge variety of plant and animal life, from the surface all the way down to the deepest trenches.

The loggerhead turtle lives in warm, shallow seas and comes ashore to lay its eggs.

The main food source in the sea is phytoplankton, a microscopic plant. Billions of phytoplankton drift near the surface of the sea, making food from sunlight, water, gases and minerals. They are the basis of the food chain* for millions of species.

Coral reefs

Coral reefs are amazing undersea structures made of the skeletons of tiny animals called coral polyps. When old polyps die, new ones grow on top of their bodies, and over many years a huge reef builds up.

Coral reefs develop in the warm, shallow seas of the tropics, and are home to the greatest variety of plant and animal life anywhere in the sea.

Part of a coral reef in the Red Sea, which lies between Egypt and Saudi Arabia

Ocean zones

The deeper down you go in the ocean, the darker and colder it is, and the fewer plants and animals are found.

Sunlit zone
Sea plants and many animals live here.

Down to 200m (650 ft)

Twilight zone
Many fish, such as swordfish, survive here.

Down to 1,000m (3,300 ft)

Sunless zone
Animals feed on dead food that falls from above.

Down to 4,000m (13,100 ft)

Abyssal zone
The water is cold and dark. Few creatures live here.

Down to 5,000m (16,400 ft)

USING SEAS AND OCEANS

For thousands of years, the sea has provided people with food. We also carry passengers and goods by sea and go on trips to the coast. But the oceans are often used as a place to dump waste, which causes pollution and may endanger wildlife.

Above and top right: the many species of sea bass are the most common fish caught and eaten around the world. These were caught in Tokyo Bay, Japan.

Fishing

Most sea fish are still caught using nets, as they have been for centuries. There are three main types of nets. Purse seine nets are drawn closed, like a purse, around schools of herring or other fish that swim near the surface. Otter trawl nets are dragged along the seabed to catch fish that live there, such as plaice, while drift or gill nets have holes just large enough for a fish to get stuck in. They are left to drift near the surface or the seabed.

Modern strong, lightweight materials mean that the nets themselves can be bigger than ever before. Fishing boats also use sonar* technology and even satellite* technology to find schools of fish.

Overfishing

Because of advances in fishing technology, fishing boats are now able to catch more fish than ever before, and the number of fish in the sea is falling rapidly. International laws have now been passed to restrict the areas where fishing boats can fish and the numbers and types of fish they can catch.

A Japanese fishing boat at work in Tokyo Bay, Japan, drawing a large net behind it.

CB3-50869

*Satellites, 11; sonar, 134

World travel

A century ago, if you wanted to travel across the sea, you had to go by boat. Huge ocean liners carried people around the world, and travel could take months.

Today, most people go long distances by plane, but boats such as ferries, hovercrafts and hydrofoils are still used for shorter distances. The only ocean liners left are cruise ships, which take people on long, relaxing sea journeys.

Container ships carry all kinds of goods in large metal boxes called containers. Cranes lift the containers off the ship quickly and transfer them to trucks or trains.

Shipping

Millions of different products, from oil and bananas to books and computers, are transported around the world on cargo ships. Ships travel more slowly than planes, but they can carry a lot more goods at once and are much cheaper to use.

Sea pollution

The seas and oceans are huge, and can absorb and break down a lot of the waste we pump into them. For example, a lot of sewage (waste from drains and toilets) goes into the sea and is broken down naturally into harmless chemicals.

However, some waste and litter doesn't break down fast enough, and ends up polluting the seas. Plastic, for example, dropped from ships or washed off beaches, can take up to 80 years to be broken down by the sea. Chemical and radioactive waste from factories, farms and nuclear power stations* can also end up in the sea and may poison plants, fish and other animals.

Oil tankers occasionally sink and spill the oil they are carrying. It can harm plants and animals, such as this seabird, by poisoning them or by coating them in oil so that they cannot breathe or move properly.

*Nuclear power, 25

Stalactites and stalagmites in The Cave of the Winds, Colorado Springs, U.S.A.

USEFUL
INFORMATION

GLOSSARY

This glossary explains some of the words you may come across when reading about the Earth. Words in *italic type* have their own entry elsewhere in the glossary.

ablation zone The lower end of a *glacier*, where the ice melts and flows into streams and rivers, or into the sea.

abyssal plain A huge, flat expanse of seabed, about 4km (2.5 miles) deep, which forms most of the ocean floor.

accumulation zone The top of a *glacier*, where snow falls and is gradually compacted into ice, which then begins to flow slowly downhill.

acid rain Rain containing dissolved chemicals from polluted air. The chemicals make the water acidic, which means it can eat away at stone and damage plant life.

active An active volcano is one which might *erupt* at any time.

adaptation The way a plant or animal *species* develops over time to suit its *habitat*.

anti-cyclone An area of high *atmospheric pressure*, which pushes winds outwards. The opposite of a *cyclone*.

aquifer A layer of *porous* rock which can hold water and carry it along under the ground.

arable Arable land is suitable for growing crops (plants). Arable farming means crop farming.

asteroid A small rock which *orbits* the Sun. Asteroids sometimes hit the Earth or other *planets*.

atmosphere A layer of gases, about 400km (250 miles) thick, that surrounds the Earth.

atmospheric pressure The pressure caused by the *atmosphere* weighing down on the Earth. It can change according to how warm the air is and how high you are above sea level.

atom A tiny particle. All *elements* are made up of atoms.

aurora Flickering lights that sometimes appear in the sky near the *North Pole* (aurora borealis) or the *South Pole* (aurora australis). Auroras are caused by *magnetic* particles from the Sun.

autonomous underwater vehicle or **AUV** A small robotic submarine which can be sent to explore the seabed by itself and bring information back to the surface.

axis The imaginary line, running from the *North Pole* to the *South Pole*, around which the Earth spins.

bacteria (singular: **bacterium**) Tiny *organisms* that live in the soil, in the air, and in plants and animals.

bedrock The solid layer of rock that lies underneath the soil, covering the Earth's surface.

biome An area with a *climate* that supports a particular range of plants and animals. For example, deserts, mountains and seas are all biomes.

black smoker A *hydrothermal vent* which churns out black water containing many dissolved minerals. The minerals gradually build up around the vent, forming a chimney.

camouflage Patterns or features (such as a tiger's stripes) which help plants and animals to look like their background and avoid being seen.

canopy The thick upper layer of leaves and branches in a rainforest.

carnivore An animal or plant that feeds on animals.

chlorofluorocarbons or **CFCs** Chemicals that are thought to damage the layer of *ozone* in the Earth's *atmosphere*.

chlorophyll A green chemical in plants which enables them to convert sunlight into food.

climate The typical or average weather conditions in a particular place. For example, the Brazilian rainforests have a very wet climate.

community The group of plants and animals that live together in a particular *habitat*.

compass A device containing a *magnetic* needle that points to the *North Pole*. A compass is used to find your direction.

conservation Protecting and preserving *environments*, including the plants, animals and buildings that form a part of them, and trying to reduce damage caused by *pollution*.

continent One of the Earth's seven major land masses.

continental crust The parts of the Earth's *crust* which form land masses. Continental crust is made mostly of a rock called granite.

continental shelf A wide shelf of seabed which surrounds most land masses, making the sea much shallower near the land than it is in the middle of the oceans.

continental slope The steep slope at the edge of the *continental shelf*, leading down to the deeper seabed.

coral polyp A small tropical sea animal. Coral polyps live together in large groups, or colonies.

coral reef A structure made up of the skeletons of *coral polyps*, built up gradually as old polyps die and new ones grow on top.

core The central part of the inside of the Earth, which scientists think is made of the metals iron and nickel.

Coriolis effect The effect of the spinning of the Earth, which forces winds and *currents* into a spiral.

crevasse A crack in a *glacier*.

crop rotation Changing the crop grown on a particular piece of land each year, to help the soil recover.

crust The Earth's solid outer layer. It consists of *continental crust* which forms the land, and *oceanic crust* which forms the seabed.

currents Global systems of water and air which are constantly circulating around the Earth. For example, the Gulf Stream is a current that carries warm water across the Atlantic Ocean from the Caribbean to northern Europe.

cyclone An area of low *atmospheric pressure*. Cyclones suck winds towards them.

debris Any kind of loose rock, mud or other matter ~ such as the rocks carried along by a *glacier*, or the material carried and *deposited* by a flowing river.

deforestation Reducing or removing forests by cutting down or burning trees.

degree One 360th of a circle. Degrees are used with *latitude* and *longitude* to measure distance on the Earth's surface. One degree is one 360th of the distance around the Earth.

delta A fan-shaped system of streams, created when a river splits up into many smaller branches and *deposits debris* as it nears the sea.

deposition Dropping or leaving behind rocks or other *debris*. For example, when *glaciers* melt, they deposit rocks as *moraine*.

desertification The process of becoming a desert.

dormant A dormant volcano is not currently *active*, but could *erupt* again. The word dormant means "sleeping".

drumlin A small hill formed from *debris deposited* by *glaciers*.

dyke A barrier built at the coast to stop the sea from flooding the land at high *tide*.

ecosystem A living system that includes a group of plants and animals and the *habitat* they live in.

element A substance made of one type of *atom*. There are over a hundred elements on Earth, such as iron, oxygen and silicon.

El Niño A weather phenomenon that sometimes makes part of the Pacific Ocean get much warmer than normal, causing severe storms.

emergent A tree that rises, or emerges, above the main *canopy* in a rainforest.

environment Surroundings, including the landscape, living things and the *atmosphere*.

Equator An imaginary line around the middle of the Earth, exactly halfway between the *North Pole* and the *South Pole*.

erratic A large boulder which has been *deposited* by a *glacier* and is left standing away from its source.

eruption A volcanic explosion. When a volcano erupts, it shoots out *lava*, rocks, hot ash and gases.

estuary A wide channel which forms where a river joins the sea.

evolution The gradual development of plants and animals, over many generations, to fit in better with their *habitats*.

exfoliation When a rock exfoliates, its outer layers peel off like layers of an onion. This is caused by changes in temperature, which make rock shrink and expand.

extinct An extinct *species* is a type of plant or animal that has died out and stopped existing. An extinct volcano is one that has stopped being *active* or *dormant* and, it is thought, will never *erupt* again.

fallow Fallow land is farmland that is being left to rest and recover between crops.

famine A widespread shortage of food, which can lead to starvation and the spread of diseases.

fault A crack in the Earth's *crust*.

fault creep The gradual movement of two pieces of the Earth's *crust* scraping against each other along a *fault*.

fertile Fertile land is land that is good for growing plants. Fertile also means able to reproduce, or have babies.

fertilizer A substance, such as *manure*, which contains *nitrates* and other chemicals and is put on land to make it more *fertile*.

fold mountains A mountain range formed by the Earth's *crust* buckling up into folds when the *plates* of the crust push together.

food chain A sequence showing which plant and animal *species* eat which.

food web A network of *food chains* showing which *species* eat each other in an *ecosystem*.

fossil The shape or remains of a plant or animal that died long ago, hardened and preserved in rock.

fossil fuels Fuels such as coal, oil and gas, made from the compressed (squashed) bodies of plants and animals that died many years ago.

freeze-thaw action The action of water which seeps into cracks in rocks and then freezes, which makes it expand (grow). This expansion forces the cracks apart, so they gradually get bigger.

fungi (singular: **fungus**) Types of *organisms*, including mushrooms, that are similar to plants but have no leaves or flowers.

galaxy A huge group of stars and planets. There are millions of galaxies in the Universe.

geology The study of the Earth's rocks and *minerals* and the way they have developed.

geostationary A word that means "in one place". Geostationary *satellites* orbit the Earth at the same speed as the Earth spins, so they always stay above the same place on the Earth's surface.

geyser A hole in the ground where water and steam, heated up inside the Earth, shoot out in bursts.

glacial valley A deep U-shaped valley carved by a flowing *glacier*, and left behind after the glacier melts.

glacier A mass of ice that gathers on top of a mountain or land mass, and flows very slowly downhill.

global warming The gradual warming-up of the Earth, possibly due to the *greenhouse effect*.

gorge A deep, narrow valley, shaped by a river gradually cutting through the land it flows across.

gravity The pulling force which holds the *atmosphere* and objects onto the Earth and stops them from floating out into space.

greenhouse effect The effect of certain gases in the *atmosphere* which trap heat from the Sun, causing the Earth to heat up.

greenhouse gases Gases, such as carbon dioxide, which contribute to the *greenhouse effect*.

groundwater Water which has soaked into the ground and is stored inside *porous* rock.

habitat The place where an animal or plant *species* lives is called its habitat.

hanging valley A smaller valley found high up the side of a *glacial valley*. Hanging valleys once contained mini-glaciers that flowed into a large glacier. When glaciers melt, hanging valleys are left behind, high up the mountainside.

heat expansion The way many substances, such as wood and rock, expand (grow) as they get warmer.

hemisphere Half of the Earth. For example, the northern hemisphere is the half that is north of the *Equator*.

herbivore An animal that eats plants.

horizons In soil science, horizons are the layers or levels found in soil. "Horizon" also means the line where you can see the land meeting the sky when you look into the distance.

hot spot A weak area of the Earth's *crust* where *magma* can break through and form a volcano.

hot spring See **thermal spring**.

humidity The amount of water contained in the air.

humus The part of soil that makes it *fertile*. Humus is made from rotted plant and animal matter.

hydroelectric power or **HEP** Power created from the energy from flowing water.

hydrothermal vent A *hot spring* on the seabed. See **black smoker**.

Ice age A period when the Earth was much colder than average. There have been several Ice ages since the Earth began.

iceberg A huge chunk of a *glacier* that has broken off into the sea. Icebergs can float far away from their glaciers and cause shipwrecks.

ice sheet A huge sheet of ice covering a large area, such as the ice that covers the *North Pole*. An ice sheet is a type of *glacier*, but flows outwards instead of downhill.

igneous Igneous rock is formed when *magma* escapes from inside the Earth, cools and hardens.

impermeable Impermeable rock is rock that does not allow water to soak through it.

infrared A type of energy which *radiates* from hot things. It is invisible to the human eye, but can be detected by infrared cameras.

intensive Intensive farming means using chemicals and technology to increase *yield*.

interglacial A period of time within an *Ice age* when the climate gets slightly warmer for a while.

isobars Lines which link points with the same *atmospheric pressure*. The isobars on a weather map show the different patterns of atmospheric pressure.

landslide A sudden slippage of rocks and soil down a hillside, often caused by heavy rain or earthquakes.

latitude A measurement of how many *degrees* a place is north or south of the *Equator*. Lines of latitude are imaginary lines around the Earth, parallel to the *Equator*.

lava Hot molten rock which bursts or flows out of volcanoes. Lava also sometimes seeps out of holes in the ground, called vents.

leap year A year every four years which has 366 days instead of 365. The extra day is always added in February, to make February 29th.

lichen A kind of living *organism* which grows on rocks, and is made up of an alga (a type of plant) and a *fungus* living together.

longitude A measurement of how many *degrees* a place is east or west of the *Prime Meridian Line*. Lines of longitude are imaginary lines that run around the Earth from north to south.

magma Hot, melted rock inside the Earth.

magnet An object that has magnetic force, an invisible force that attracts iron and steel. The two ends of a magnet are known as its poles.

magnetic poles The Earth behaves like a giant *magnet*, and the ends of this magnet are called the magnetic poles. They move gradually over time, and are not in exactly the same place as the geographic *North Pole* and *South Pole*.

malaria A dangerous disease, which affects millions of people, spread by insects called mosquitoes.

mantle The thick layer of rock under the Earth's *crust*. Some of it is solid and some is *magma* (molten rock).

manure Animal dung which can be used as a *fertilizer*.

meander A bend or long loop in a river. Meanders form when rivers flow across gently sloping land.

Mediterranean A type of climate that has warm winters and hot summers, and is good for growing many types of crops. It is named after the region around the Mediterranean Sea, but is also found in other parts of the world.

megacity A name for a city that has more than a million people.

metamorphic Metamorphic rocks have been changed by heat or pressure. For example, when a rock called shale is squashed, it hardens into a type of metamorphic rock called slate.

meteorology The study of the weather and how to predict it.

migration Moving from one place to another. Many animals migrate each season to find food.

mineral A non-living substance found in the Earth, such as salt, iron, diamond or quartz. Most rocks are made up of a mixture of minerals.

mirage An image of something that is somewhere else, caused by light bending in the *atmosphere*.

molecule Two or more *atoms* bonded together. Many substances are made up of molecules.

monsoon A season of strong winds and heavy rain which affects some areas of Asia.

moon A natural *satellite orbiting* around a *planet*. The Earth has one moon which orbits it once a month.

moraine Boulders, clay and other *debris* left behind by a *glacier*.

natural selection The theory that those animals and plants that are best suited to their *environment* are the most likely to survive.

navigable A navigable river is one that ships can travel along.

niche A particular plant or animal *species'* place in an *ecosystem*.

nitrates Chemicals found in soil that help plants to grow.

Northern Lights See **aurora borealis.**

North Pole The most northern point on the Earth, and one end of the *axis* the Earth spins around.

nuclear power Energy produced by splitting *atoms* of a *radioactive element* called uranium.

oasis A *fertile* area in a desert, supplied by water from an *aquifer*.

oceanic crust The parts of the Earth's *crust* which form the seabed. Oceanic crust is made mostly of a rock called basalt.

oceanic ridge A raised ridge on the seabed, caused by the *plates* of the Earth's *crust* pulling apart and *magma* pushing up in between.

oceanic trench A deep trench in the seabed that forms where one *plate* pushes underneath another.

oceanography The study of seas and oceans.

omnivore An animal that eats both meat and plants. Omnivore means "everything-eater".

orbit The path of one object as it travels around, or orbits, another. For example, the Earth orbits the Sun once a year.

ore Rock which contains metal that can be extracted. For example, iron is often extracted from an iron ore called haematite.

organic Organic farming means farming without artificial chemicals and methods. Organic food is food that has been produced in this way and contains no artificial chemicals.

organism A living thing, such as a plant, animal or *bacterium*.

outcrop A rocky piece of land that stands out from the surrounding area.

oxbow lake A curved lake left behind when a river *meander* gets cut off from the rest of the river.

ozone A type of oxygen in which each molecule contains three oxygen atoms instead of two.

ozone layer A layer of *ozone* in the Earth's atmosphere, from 20 to 50km (12 to 30 miles) above the Earth's surface, which protects the Earth from the Sun's rays. The ozone layer may be being damaged by *chlorofluorocarbons* or *CFCs*.

Pangaea The name scientists give to a huge continent that they think once existed on Earth. It gradually broke up to form the *continents* we have today.

pastoral Pastoral farming means raising and breeding animals.

permafrost A layer of ice that never melts. It is found underneath the soil in *Arctic* areas.

photosynthesis A chemical process in plants, which converts sunlight into food.

planet A large ball of rock which *orbits* a *star*. For example, Earth and Mars are planets which orbit the Sun.

plates The separate pieces of *crust* which fit together like a jigsaw puzzle to cover the Earth.

plate tectonics The theory that the *plates* of the Earth's *crust* gradually move around and rub against each other.

poles The *North Pole* and the *South Pole*, the coldest parts of the Earth which are farthest away from the *Equator*.

pollution Waste or dirt, such as exhaust from cars, which builds up faster than it can be broken down.

population The number of people living in a particular place.

porous Able to soak up water. Porous rock can soak up water like a sponge and store it underground.

port A town or city where ships can load and unload.

precipitation Rain, snow, hail or any other water falling from the sky.

Prime Meridian Line An imaginary line that runs from north to south through Greenwich, England, at zero *degrees* of *longitude*.

projection The way the curved surface of the Earth is distorted (stretched) so that it can be shown on a flat map.

radar A system that detects objects such as clouds by sending out radio waves and collecting the signals that bounce back. Radar stands for **RA**dio **D**etecting **A**nd **R**anging.

radiation Energy, such as light, heat or *radioactive* particles, that radiates (flows outwards) from an energy source. For example, the Sun radiates light and heat.

radioactive Radioactive substances, such as uranium, give off particles which can be harmful.

remote-operated vehicle or **ROV** A remote-controlled robot used for exploring the seabed.

remote sensing Recording information from a long distance away; for example, measuring sea temperatures from a *satellite*.

rift valley A valley formed on land where two *plates* of the Earth's *crust* pull away from each other.

Ring of Fire A group of volcanoes and *faults* that forms a huge ring around the Pacific Ocean.

satellite An object that *orbits* a *planet*. Many satellites are built to do particular jobs, such as monitoring the weather.

sedimentary Sedimentary rock is rock made up of particles of sand, mud and other *debris* that have settled on the seabed and been squashed down to form hard rock.

seismology The study of earthquakes and other, smaller movements of the Earth.

selective breeding Developing plants and animals by choosing those with good qualities for farming.

sewage Waste and dirty water from sinks and bathrooms.

shanty town A makeshift town that grows up on the outskirts of overpopulated cities, when people build their own homes out of junk.

slash-and-burn A method of destroying trees quickly to make room for farmland.

smog A mixture of smoke and fog. Also a general word for *pollution*.

solar system The Sun and the *planets* and *satellites*, including the Earth, that *orbit* it.

solar year The amount of time it takes the Earth to *orbit* the Sun once. A solar year is about 365¼ days.

sonar A method of bouncing sounds off objects and measuring the results in order to make maps. Sonar is used to map the seabed.

South Pole The most southern point on the Earth, and one end of the *axis* the Earth spins around.

species (plural: **species**) A type of plant, animal or other living thing.

stalactites Columns of stone that hang down inside caves, made by water dripping from the cave roof and *depositing* dissolved minerals.

stalagmites Towers of stone which rise from the ground in caves, formed by water dripping onto the cave floor and *depositing* dissolved minerals.

star A huge ball of burning gas in space. The Sun, in the middle of our *solar system*, is a star.

stomata (singular: **stoma**) Tiny holes in leaves that allow gases and water in and out. See **transpiration**.

strata (singular: **stratum**) Layers of rock.

subduction zone An area of the seabed where one *plate* of the Earth's crust plunges underneath another, forming a deep trench.

submersible A small submarine used by scientists to explore the seabed.

subsoil A layer of rough soil underneath the *topsoil*. The rocks and cracks in subsoil help water to drain through it.

temperate A mild, damp *climate*, between extremes of hot and cold.

terraces Large steps dug into hill-sides to hold soil and water in place for farming.

thermal spring A place where hot water, heated by underground rocks, comes to the surface of the Earth. Also known as a hot spring.

tidal wave Very large waves are sometimes called tidal waves. However, *tsunamis* are not tidal waves, as they are caused by underwater volcanoes or earthquakes and have nothing to do with tides.

tides The daily movement of the sea up and down the shore, caused by the gravity of the *moon*.

topsoil The rich, uppermost layer of soil. It contains *humus* and various *organisms* which make soil *fertile*.

transpiration A process that takes place in plants. Water that the plant has sucked in through its roots travels up to the plant's leaves, and transpires, or evaporates, out through the *stomata*.

treeline The height up a mountain after which there are no more trees (because it is too cold and windy for them to survive).

tributary A river that flows into a bigger river, instead of into the sea.

tropics The warm, wet areas on either side of the *Equator*.

tsunami A giant wave caused by an earthquake or volcano on the seabed making the water vibrate.

tundra A type of land in which the soil is always partly frozen. It is found in the *Arctic*.

turbine A machine that converts turning power (such as the spinning of a waterwheel) into electricity.

ultraviolet or **UV** A type of invisible light *radiation* from the Sun which can cause skin damage.

understorey The level of a rainforest where small trees and plants grow, between the *canopy* and the forest floor.

vulcanology The study of volcanoes.

water table The top level of the *groundwater* that is stored in underground rock.

yield The amount of food or other produce that is grown on a particular piece of land.

MAPS AND LINES

The Earth is a huge, round ball of rock moving through space. It has no "top" or "bottom" and no lines marked on it. Lines such as the Equator, the Arctic Circle and the International Date Line, which are explained here, are all imaginary. They are used to help us measure distances and find places on maps.

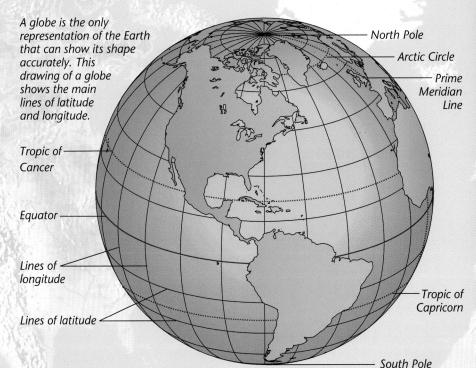

A globe is the only representation of the Earth that can show its shape accurately. This drawing of a globe shows the main lines of latitude and longitude.

North Pole
Arctic Circle
Prime Meridian Line
Tropic of Cancer
Equator
Lines of longitude
Lines of latitude
Tropic of Capricorn
South Pole

What do the lines mean?

• **Lines of latitude**, or **parallels**, run around the globe, dividing it into flat slices. Lines of latitude get shorter the closer they are to the poles, but they never meet each other.

• The **Equator** is the biggest and most important line of latitude. It runs around the globe halfway between the North Pole and the South Pole. The other lines of latitude are measured north and south from it.

• **Lines of longitude**, also known as **meridians**, run from the North Pole to the South Pole, dividing the globe into segments, like the segments of an orange. They all meet at the North Pole and at the South Pole.

• The **Prime Meridian Line** is the most important line of longitude, because all the other lines are measured from it. But it is not longer than any of the others; the lines are all the same size. It was decided in 1884 that the Prime Meridian would run through Greenwich, near London in England.

• **Degrees** (°) are used to measure distance on the globe. One degree is one 360th of the way around the globe. Lines of latitude are measured in degrees north and south of the Equator, while lines of longitude are measured in degrees east and west of the Prime Meridian Line. For example, somewhere that is 50°S and 100°E has a latitude 50 degrees south of the Equator, and a longitude 100 degrees east of the Prime Meridian Line.

• **Minutes** (') and **seconds** (") are smaller distances, used for making more precise measurements. There are 60 minutes in one degree, and 60 seconds in one minute.

• The **Arctic Circle** is a line of latitude at 66°30' north. The area north of it includes the North Pole and is known as the **Arctic**.

• The **Antarctic Circle** is a line of latitude at 66°30' south. It contains the South Pole and the area south of it is known as the **Antarctic**.

• The **tropics** are two lines of latitude near the Equator. The **Tropic of Cancer** is at 23°27' north and the **Tropic of Capricorn** is at 23°27' south. The hot, stormy area that lies between these two lines is also sometimes known as the **tropics**.

• The **International Date Line** is near the 180th meridian (the line at 180° longitude, directly opposite the Prime Meridian Line). It runs mostly through the Pacific Ocean, and is not straight but bends to avoid the land. It is part of the system that is used to define international time zones (see opposite). The date changes from one side of the line to the other.

Map projections

A flat map cannot show the world as it really is. So, to represent the round Earth on a flat surface, it has to be distorted (stretched) or divided into pieces. Some methods of doing this, called projections, are shown here.

• A **cylindrical projection** is similar to what you would get if you wrapped a piece of paper around a globe to form a cylinder, then shone a light inside the globe. The shapes of the countries would be projected onto the paper. Near the Equator they would be accurate, but near the poles they would look distorted.

A cylindrical map projection

• In the **Robinson projection**, the longitude lines curve in at the poles, so countries in the far north and south don't look too big. The curved lines can be confusing, but the map represents the Earth's proportions quite well.

The Robinson map projection

• The **Peters projection** stretches the countries near to the Equator, so that all the countries are the right size in relation to each other. But this makes them look too long, so they aren't the right shape.

The Peters map projection

• The **Homosline projection** splits the globe up into sections. It makes each country almost the right shape and size, but it's not very useful for working out distances and routes, especially if you live near one of the edges!

The Homosline map projection

• The **Mercator projection** is probably the most well-known projection. It was invented by Gerardus Mercator in 1538. It is like a cylindrical projection, but is stretched out at the poles. The countries are the right shape, but those nearest the poles look too big.

The Mercator map projection

Time zones

Because the sun rises and sets at different times across the world, the Earth is divided into 24 time zones. In each zone, people set their clocks to their own standard time. There is a new zone every 15 degrees of longitude, but this is only a rough guide, as whole countries or states usually keep to the same local time instead of sticking to the zones exactly. In some countries, they use a different Summer Time. This map shows how the time zones work. The zones are measured in hours ahead of or behind Greenwich Mean Time, or GMT, which is the time at the Prime Meridian Line.

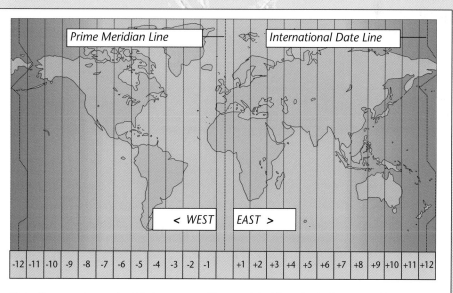

This diagram shows the 24 time zones. The areas ahead of GMT meet the areas behind GMT at the International Date Line (on the opposite side of the world from the Prime Meridian Line). If you travel east across the International Date Line, you go back 24 hours. If you travel west across it, you go forward 24 hours.

THE EARTH'S CYCLES

The Earth is constantly going through repeated processes, or cycles, such as the orbit of the Earth around the Sun, the way it spins and tilts as it moves through space, the orbit of the Moon around the Earth, and the sequence of the tides.

Days and years

Days and years are created by the movement of the Earth in relation to the Sun. Here are some facts and figures about the Earth's orbit.

• One **day** is the amount of time it takes the Earth to spin around on its axis. We divide each day into 24 hours of 60 minutes each.

• The exact amount of time it takes the Earth to make one complete orbit around the Sun is 365.26 days. This is known as a **solar year**.

• Instead of having 365.26 days, a normal **year** on Earth has exactly 365 days (because this is easier for us). Every four years another day is added to make up the difference. A year with an extra day in it is called a **leap year**. The extra day is added to February, so in leap years February has 29 days instead of 28.

• Making every fourth year a leap year does not even things out exactly, so some leap years are missed. Usually, every fourth year is a leap year, such as 1988, 1992 and 1996. But century years, such as 1700, 1800 and 1900, are not leap years. However, millenium years, such as the year 2000, *are* leap years.

Calendars

A **calendar** is a system of measuring years, months, weeks and days. People don't all agree when the world began, so years cannot be measured from then. Several different calendars, mostly based on religious beliefs, are used today.

Years ago	Christian Calendar	Muslim Calendar	Chinese Calendar	Hebrew Calendar
5,800				
5,600				*This is when Hebrews believe the world began.*
5,400				
5,200				
5,000				
4,800				
4,600				
4,400			*Emperor Huang Di is said to have invented the Chinese calendar 4,600 years ago.*	
4,200				
4,000				
3,800				
3,600				
3,400				
3,200				
3,000				
2,800				
2,600				
2,400				
2,200				
2,000				
1,800	*The Christian calendar begins with the birth of Christ, the founder of Christianity.*			
1,600				
1,400				
1,200		*This is when the Muslim prophet Mohammed fled from Mecca to Medina.*		
1,000				
800				
600				
400				
200				
0				

This chart shows how many years ago the different calendars began. When the Christian calendar is on the year 2000, the Muslim calendar is on the year 1378, and so on.

The Moon

A **moon** is a ball of rock orbiting (moving around) a planet. The Earth only has one moon, but some planets have more. Jupiter, for example, has at least 16 moons.

Our Moon orbits the Earth once every 27 days, 7 hours and 43 minutes. The Moon "shines" because it is reflecting light from the Sun. Whether we see a full moon, a thin crescent moon, or something in between, depends on what position the Moon is in and how much sunlight it can reflect onto the Earth. These different shapes are called the phases of the Moon.

This diagram shows the phases of the Moon as it orbits the Earth.

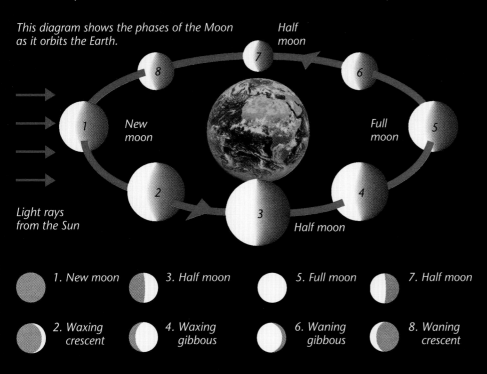

Half moon

New moon

Full moon

Light rays from the Sun

Half moon

1. New moon

2. Waxing crescent

3. Half moon

4. Waxing gibbous

5. Full moon

6. Waning gibbous

7. Half moon

8. Waning crescent

Phases of the Moon

• A **new moon** does not shine at all. The Moon's cycle begins when the Moon is between the Earth and the Sun, so none of the light it reflects can reach the Earth.

• A **half moon** appears when the Moon has moved around and is alongside the Earth. We see half of it reflecting the Sun.

• A **full moon** is what you see when the Moon is on the opposite side of the Earth from the Sun. All the sunlight the Moon reflects can be seen from the Earth, so the Moon looks like a complete circle.

More Moon facts

• When the Moon is moving away from the Sun and growing fuller, it is **waxing**. When it moves around towards the Sun again and seems to be getting smaller, it is **waning**.

• A **crescent moon** is between a new moon and a half moon, and looks like a crescent or C-shape.

• A **gibbous moon** is between a half moon and a full moon, and is a fat oval shape.

• A **lunar month** is the amount of time it takes the Moon to complete its cycle: 29 days, 12 hours and 44 minutes. This is longer than the orbit time, because while the Moon is making its orbit around the Earth, the Earth is moving around the Sun and so changing its own position.

• Like the Earth, the Moon spins around on its axis. It does this every 27 days, 7 hours and 43 minutes. This is exactly the same amount of time as the time it takes to travel around the Earth, which means we always see the same side of the Moon from Earth. However, we can see the other side of the Moon in pictures taken by spacecraft.

• The Moon is 3,476km (2,160 miles) across, about a quarter of the width of the Earth. Its circumference is 10,927km (6,790 miles) and its distance away from the Earth varies between 356,399 and 384,403 km (221,456 and 238,857 miles). It orbits the Earth at about 3,700 km/hr (2,300 miles per hour).

• A **month** on Earth is a period of time based on the Moon's cycle. But to make 12 months fit into a year, an average month is about 30 days long, slightly longer than a lunar month.

• A **blue moon** happens when there are two full moons within one Earth month. The second full moon of the two is called the blue moon.

Tides

The water in the Earth's seas and oceans rises and falls twice a day. These movements are called tides, and they are caused by the gravity of the Moon.

As the Earth spins, different parts of its surface move past the Moon. The part nearest the Moon has a high tide, when the water rises as the Moon pulls it.

At the same time, a high tide also happens on the opposite side of the Earth, because of a reaction called centrifugal force, created by the way the Earth and the Moon move around each other.

While this is happening, there is a low tide on the parts of the Earth's surface that are not facing or opposite the Moon. Each part of the world has two high tides and two low tides every day.

SCIENCES AND SCIENTISTS

Many scientists are involved in studying all the different aspects of the Earth. The sciences that relate to the Earth are often called the Earth sciences or geosciences. *Geo* is Greek for "Earth", and it appears in the names of many of these sciences.

The table below shows some of the Earth sciences and the scientists who study them, and describes which area each science deals with. Some of the sciences overlap; for example, geologists and paleontologists may both study fossils.

Science	Name of scientist	What is it?
Geography	Geographer	The study of the Earth's features and processes, climates, resources, maps, and the way people relate to the Earth.
Geology	Geologist	The study of the rocks the Earth is made of and how they formed.
Paleontology	Paleontologist	The study of fossils and the organisms that formed them.
Mineralogy	Mineralogist	The study of minerals.
Geophysics	Geophysicist	The study of the forces that affect the Earth, such as its magnetic field, its movement through space, and gravity.
Geochemistry	Geochemist	The study of the Earth's chemicals and how they occur naturally, both on the Earth's surface and inside the Earth.
Geomorphology	Geomorphologist	The study of landforms, or the shapes and features on the Earth's surface, and the processes which cause them.
Vulcanology	Vulcanologist	The study of volcanoes.
Seismology	Seismologist	The study of earthquakes and earth tremors.
Oceanography	Oceanographer	The study of seas and oceans and the seabed.
Sedimentology	Sedimentologist	The study of sedimentary deposits ~ layers of rock, minerals, mud or other substances which have settled on land or on the seabed.
Meteorology	Meteorologist	The study of the weather and weather forecasting.
Climatology	Climatologist	The study of climates past and present.
Ecology	Ecologist	The study of the relationship between living things (including humans) and their surroundings on Earth.
Pedology	Pedologist	The study of soil. This is also often known as soil science.
Cartography	Cartographer	The science of designing and making maps, and collecting the information needed to make them.

Earth scientists

These are some of the famous scientists who have contributed to our understanding of how the Earth and its processes work.

Agricola, Georgius (1494-1555)
German scientist who studied rocks and minerals scientifically, at a time when most theories about what they were made of were based on superstition. His book *De Re Metallica* (1556) was a guide for miners and geologists.

al-Idrisi (c.1100- c.1165)
Arabic geographer and author who explored the Mediterranean region, created an early map of the world, and wrote a book, *The Book of Roger*, describing his travels.

Aristotle (384BC-322BC)
Greek scientist and philosopher who wrote on many subjects. He realized that the Earth was a sphere, although it took a long time for everyone to accept this. (Until about 1500AD, many people still thought the Earth was flat.)

Darwin, Charles (1809-1882)
English scientist who developed the theory of natural selection, which argues that plant and animal species change, or evolve, over long periods of time. This theory was controversial, partly because it suggested that the Earth was much older than many people believed.

Davis, William Morris (1850-1934)
American geologist and meteorologist who founded the science of geomorphology. He developed a theory of how the process of erosion forms a cycle and was famous for his detailed diagrams showing how features of the Earth's crust are formed.

Democritus (c.460BC-c.370BC)
Greek philosopher who was the first to claim that all matter was made up of tiny particles, or atoms. He also studied earthquakes, volcanoes, the water cycle and erosion.

Eratosthenes (c.276BC-c.196BC)
Greek scientist and geographer who made the first measurement of the distance around the Earth, using the stars as a guide.

Flammarion, Camille (1842-1925)
French astronomer who wrote and illustrated a popular book about the weather, *L'Atmosphère* (The Atmosphere, 1872) which was translated into many languages. Flammarion's picture of waterspouts is reproduced on page 85 of this book.

Gardner, Julia Anna (1882-1960)
American geologist and paleontologist. Her studies of fossils were important because they increased understanding of rock layers, or strata.

Gould, Stephen Jay (born 1941)
American geologist and paleontologist who built on the theories of Charles Darwin. He has written many popular books such as *Wonderful Life* (1989).

Henry the Navigator (1394-1460)
A prince of Portugal who planned and paid for many journeys of exploration to Africa. He opened a school which taught explorers how to navigate (find their way) and record their discoveries.

Humboldt, Alexander von (1769-1859)
German explorer who contributed to the sciences of geography, geology, meteorology and oceanography. He explored South America and wrote a 5-volume book, *Kosmos* (The Cosmos), in 1844, describing the geography and geology of the world.

Hutton, James (1726-1797)
Scottish scientist who studied rocks and minerals, and is sometimes called "the father of geology". He said that the Earth's crust changed gradually through erosion, volcanic eruptions and other processes.

Lyell, Sir Charles (1797-1875)
Scottish geologist who developed the theories of James Hutton. He was also a friend of Charles Darwin and his ideas helped Darwin with his theory of natural selection.

Ptolemy (c.100AD-c.170AD)
Egyptian geographer and astronomer. He devised an early system of latitude and longitude and used it to create many maps.

Schmitt, Harrison Hagan (born 1935)
American geologist and astronaut who was on the Apollo 17 mission to the Moon in 1972. He is famous for his 22-hour journey in a moon buggy to collect geological samples ~ the longest trip ever made on the Moon.

Torricelli, Evangelista (1608-1647)
Italian mathematician and physicist who studied atmospheric pressure. In 1643, he invented the barometer (an instrument that measures atmospheric pressure).

Varenius, Bernhardus (1622-1650)
German geographer. He wrote a major book, *Geographia Generalis* (General Geography) in 1650, and also studied the islands of Japan.

Wegener, Alfred (1880-1930)
German meteorologist who claimed that all the Earth's continents had once been joined together in one big continent, which he named Pangaea. Wegener's theories were not accepted at the time, but were used in the 1960s when they helped scientists develop the theory of plate tectonics, about how the Earth's continents have moved.

WORLD RECORDS

Here are some of the Earth's longest rivers, highest mountains and other amazing world records. But, the world is always changing; mountains wear down, rivers change shape, and new buildings are constructed. Ways of measuring things can also change. That's why you may find slightly different figures in different books.

Highest mountains	
Everest, Nepal/China border	8,848m (29,028 ft)
K2, Pakistan/China border	8,611m (28,250 ft)
Makalu, Nepal/China border	8,470m (27,789 ft)
Dhaulagiri, Nepal	8,172m (26,810 ft)
Nanga Parbat, Pakistan	8,126m (26,660 ft)
Annapurna, Nepal	8,078m (26,504 ft)
Rakaposhi, Pakistan	7,788m (25,550 ft)
Kongur Shan, China	7,719m (25,325 ft)
Tirich Mir, Pakistan	7,690m (25,230 ft)
Gongga Shan, China	7,556m (24,790 ft)

Longest rivers	
Nile, Africa	6,671km (4,145 miles)
Amazon, South America	6,440km (4,000 miles)
Chang Jiang, China	6,276 km (3,900 miles)
Mississippi, U.S.A.	6,019km (3,741 miles)
Ob'/Irtysh/Black Irtysh, Asia	5,411km (3,362 miles)
Yenisey/Angara, Russia	4,989km (3,100 miles)
Huang He, China	4,630km (2,877 miles)
Amur/Shilka/Onon, Asia	4,416km (2,744 miles)
Lena, Russia	4,400km (2,734 miles)
Congo, Africa	4,374km (2,718 miles)

Biggest natural lakes	
Caspian Sea, Asia	370,999km² (143,243 mi²)
Lake Superior, U.S.A./Canada	82,414km² (31,820 mi²)
Lake Victoria, Africa	69,215km² (26,724 mi²)
Lake Huron, U.S.A./Canada	59,596km² (23,010 mi²)
Lake Michigan, U.S.A	58,016km² (22,400 mi²)
Aral Sea, Asia	41,000km² (15,830 mi²)
Lake Tanganyika, Africa	32,764km² (12,650 mi²)
Lake Baykal, Russia	31,500km² (12,162 mi²)
Great Bear Lake, Canada	31,328km² (12,096 mi²)
Lake Nyasa, Africa	29,928km² (11,555 mi²)

Deepest ocean
The Marianas Trench, part of the Pacific Ocean, is the deepest part of the sea at 11,033m (36,198 ft) deep.

Deepest lake
Lake Baykal in Russia is the deepest lake in the world. At its deepest point it is 1,620m (5,316 ft) deep.

Biggest islands	
Greenland	2,175,600km² (840,000 mi²)
New Guinea	789,950km² (305,000 mi²)
Borneo	751,100km² (290,000 mi²)
Madagascar	586,376km² (226,400 mi²)
Baffin Island, Canada	507,454km² (195,928 mi²)
Sumatra, Indonesia	424,760km² (164,000 mi²)
Honshu, Japan	227,920km² (88,000 mi²)
Great Britain	218,896km² (84,400 mi²)
Victoria Island, Canada	217,290km² (83,896 mi²)
Ellesmere Island, Canada	196,236km² (75,767 mi²)

Tallest buildings	
Petronas Towers, Malaysia	452m (1,483 ft)
Sears Tower, U.S.A.	443m (1,454 ft)
Jin Mao Building, China	420m (1,379 ft
World Trade Center, U.S.A.	417m (1,368 ft)
Empire State Building, U.S.A.	381m (1,250 ft)
Central Plaza, China	374m (1,227 ft)
Bank of China, China	369m (1,209 ft)
The Center, China	350m (1,148 ft)
T&C Tower, Taiwan	347m (1,140 ft)
Amoco Building, U.S.A.	346m (1,136 ft)

Biggest cities and urban areas	
Tokyo-Yokohama, Japan	26.6 million
New York City, U.S.A.	16.3 million
São Paulo, Brazil	16.2 million
Mexico City, Mexico	15.6 million
Shanghai, China	14.8 million
Bombay, India	14.5 million
Los Angeles, U.S.A.	12.3 million
Beijing, China	12.1 million
Calcutta, India	11.5 million
Seoul, South Korea	11.5 million

Famous waterfalls	Height
Angel Falls, Venezuela	979m (3,212 ft)
Sutherland Falls, New Zealand	580m (1,904 ft)
Mardalfossen, Norway	517m (1,696 ft)
Falls of Gersoppa, India	253m (830 ft)
Victoria Falls, Zimbabwe/Zambia	108m (355 ft)
Iguacu Falls, Brazil/Argentina	82m (269 ft)
Niagara Falls, Canada/U.S.A.	54m (176 ft)

Natural disasters

Natural disasters can be measured in different ways. For example, some earthquakes score highly on the Richter scale, while others cause more destruction. The earthquakes, volcanic eruptions, floods, hurricanes and tornadoes listed here are among the most famous and destructive disasters in history.

Earthquakes	Richter scale	Disastrous effects
Shansi, China, 1556	unknown	830,000 people were killed
Calcutta, India, 1737	unknown	300,000 deaths
San Francisco, U.S.A., 1906	8.3	3,000 people died in resulting fire
Messina, Italy, 1908	7.5	Over 70,000 people died
Quetta, Pakistan, 1935	7.5	Up to 60,000 people died
Alaska, U.S.A., 1964	9.2	131 people died in this huge quake
Tangshan, China, 1976	8.0	Over 250,000 people died
Mexico City, Mexico, 1985	8.1	10,000 died, with $5bn damage
Iran, 1990	7.7	50,000 people died
Kobe, Japan, 1995	7.7	5,500 killed, over $147bn damage

Volcanic eruptions	Disastrous effects
Mount Vesuvius, Italy, 79AD	Town of Pompeii flattened; 3,400 died
Tambora, Indonesia, 1815	92,000 people starved to death
Krakatau, Indonesia, 1883	36,500 drowned in resulting tsunami
Mount Pelee, Martinique, 1902	Nearly 30,000 people buried in ash flows
Kelut, Indonesia, 1919	Over 5,000 people drowned in mud
Agung, Indonesia, 1963	1,200 people suffocated in hot ash
Mount St. Helens, U.S.A., 1980	Only 61 died but a large area was destroyed
Ruiz, Colombia, 1985	25,000 people died in giant mud flows
Mount Pinatubo, Chile, 1991	800 killed by collapsing roofs and disease
Island of Montserrat, 1995	Volcano left most of the island uninhabitable

Floods	Disastrous effects
Holland, 1220	100,000 drowned by a sea flood
Kaifeng, China, 1642	300,000 died after rebels destroyed a dyke
Johnstown, U.S.A., 1889	2,200 killed in a flood caused by rain
Fréjus, France, 1959	412 died after Malpasset Dam burst
Italy, 1963	Vaoint Dam overflowed; up to 4,000 killed
East Pakistan, 1970	Giant wave caused by cyclone killed 200,000
Bangladesh, 1988	1,300 died, 30m homeless in monsoon flood
Southern U.S.A., 1993	$12bn of damage after Mississippi flooded
China, 1998	Yangtze overflow left 14m homeless
Papua New Guinea, 1998	3 tsunamis swamped Sepik and killed 2,000

Storms	Disastrous effects
Caribbean "Great Hurricane," 1780	Biggest ever hurricane killed over 20,000
Hong Kong typhoon, China, 1906	10,000 people died in this giant hurricane
Killer tornado, U.S.A., 1925	689 people killed in Ellington, Missouri
Tropical Storm Agnes, U.S.A., 1972	$3.5bn damage to U.S.A.'s East coast, 129 dead
Hurricane Fifi, Honduras, 1974	8,000 people died and 100,000 left homeless
Hurricane Georges, U.S.A., 1998	Southern U.S.A. hit; $5bn of damage
Hurricane Mitch, C. America, 1998	Over 9,000 killed across Central America

Amazing Earth facts

The Earth is 12,103km (7,520 miles) across. Its circumference (the distance around the Equator) is 38,022km (23,627 miles) and it is 149,503,000 km (92,897,000 miles) away from the Sun.

To make one complete orbit around the Sun, the Earth has to travel 938,900,000km (583,400,000 miles). To do this in just a year, it has to travel very fast. Because of the atmosphere surrounding the Earth, you can't feel it moving. But in fact you are zooming through space faster than any rocket.

- **Orbit speed** The Earth travels around the Sun at about 106,000 km/hr (65,868 miles per hour).

- **Spinning speed** The Earth also spins around an axis, but the speed you are spinning at depends on where you live. Places on the Equator move at 1600km/hr (995 miles per hour). New York City moves at around 1100 km/hr (684 miles per hour). Near the poles, the spinning is not very fast at all. (You can see how this works by looking at a spinning globe.)

- **Solar system speed** The whole solar system, including the Sun, the Earth and its moon, and the other planets and their moons, is moving at 72,400 km/hr (45,000 miles per hour) through the galaxy.

- **Galaxy speed** Our galaxy, the Milky Way, whizzes through the universe at 2,172,150 km/hr (1,350,000 miles per hour).

MEASUREMENTS

Measuring things ~ distance, area, weight, volume, time and temperature ~ is one of the most important parts of science. There are two main systems of measurement: metric and imperial. This page shows how each measuring system works, and also how to convert from one into the other.

Imperial

This system of measurement is very old, dating from the 12th century or even earlier. It can be hard to use because it is not based on the decimal (base 10) system which we use for numbers. Some of the units have symbols or abbreviations. For example, the symbol for an inch is ".

Length and distance

12 inches (") = 1 foot (')
3 feet = 1 yard (yd)
1,760 yards = 1 mile
3 miles = 1 league

Area

144 square inches = 1 square foot
9 square feet = 1 square yard
4840 square yards = 1 acre
640 acres = 1 square mile

Weight

16 drams (dr) = 1 ounce (oz)
16 ounces = 1 pound (lb)
14 pounds = 1 stone
2240 pounds (160 stone) = 1 ton
2,000 pounds = 1 short ton

Volume and capacity

1,728 cubic inches = 1 cubic foot (ft^3)
27 cubic feet = 1 cubic yard (yd^3)
5 fluid ounces (fl oz) = 1 gill (gi)

20 fluid ounces = 1 pint (pt) (U.K.)
16 fluid ounces = 1 pint (U.S.)
2 pints = 1 quart (qt)
8 pints (4 quarts) = 1 gallon (gal)

Temperature

The imperial unit of temperature is one degree (°) Fahrenheit (F). The freezing point of water is 32° F and the boiling point of water is 212° F.

Metric

The metric or decimal system is based on the metre or meter, a unit of measurement which was first used in France in the 1790s. Metric units are multiples of each other by 10, 100 or 1000. Countries around the world are gradually switching from imperial to metric. Many of the metric units have both U.S. spellings (-er) and European spellings (-re).

Length and distance

10 millimeters/millimetres (mm) =
        1 centimeter/centimetre (cm)
100 cm = 1 meter/metre (m)
1,000 m = 1 kilometer/kilometre (km)

Area

100 square mm (mm^2) =
        1 square cm (cm^2)
10,000 square cm =
        1 square m (m^2)
10,000 square m = 1 hectare
1,000,000 square m = 1 square
        kilometer/kilometre (km^2)

Weight

1,000 grams (g) = 1 kilogram (kg)
1,000 kilograms = 1 tonne (t)

Volume and capacity

1 cubic cm (cc or cm^3) = 1
        milliliter/millilitre (ml)
1,000 ml = 1 liter/litre (l)
1,000 l = 1 cubic m (m^3)

Temperature

The metric temperature unit is one degree (°) Celsius (C). Water freezes at 0°C and boils at 100° C.

Conversion tables

You can convert between metric and imperial with this table. Use a calculator to do the multiplications.

To convert	into	multiply by
cm	inches	0.394
m	yards	1.094
km	miles	0.621
grams	ounces	0.35
kilograms	pounds	2.205
tonnes	tons	0.984
cm^2	square inches	0.155
m^2	square yards	1.196
km^2	square miles	0.386
hectares	acres	2.471
liters/litres	pints	1.76
inches	cm	2.54
yards	m	0.914
miles	km	1.609
ounces	grams	28.35
pounds	kilograms	0.454
tons	tonnes	1.016
square inches	cm^2	6.452
square yards	m^2	0.836
square miles	km^2	2.59
acres	hectares	0.405
pints	liters/litres	0.5683

USEFUL ADDRESSES

Here is a list of organizations involved with Earth-related subjects. They may be able to provide information to help with projects. If you have access to a computer with an Internet connection, you can also look for information on the World Wide Web. The Web sites listed here will help you get started.

Organizations

The United Kingdom Met. Office produces weather forecasts. Its education service provides a range of useful information.

> The Met Office Education Service
> Sutton House, London Road
> Bracknell RG12 2SY, U.K.

The Woods Hole Oceanographic Institute is one of the world's biggest sea and ocean research institutes. It conducts studies all over the world.

> Information Office, Woods Hole
> Oceanographic Institute
> Woods Hole, MA 02543, U.S.A.

The National Geographic Society promotes the study of geography through its magazines *National Geographic* and *National Geographic World*, books, TV films, maps and information packs.

> National Geographic Society
> 1145 17th Street N.W.
> Washington D.C. 20036, U.S.A.

The Natural Environment Research Council runs studies on the environment and can help schools by providing information.

> National Environmental Research
> Council Schools Programme
> Polaris House, North Star Avenue
> Swindon SN2 1EU, U.K.

The U.N. Information Centre can help you with subjects such as population, agriculture and industry.

> U.N. Information Centre
> Millbank Tower 21st Floor
> 21-24 Millbank
> London SW1P 4QH, U.K.

Web sites

General geography and Earth science sites
National Geographic	http://www.nationalgeographic.com/
NASA	http://www.nasa.gov/
Discovery Channel	http://www.discovery.com/
U.S. Geological Survey	http://www.usgs.gov/
Earth Science Explorer	http://www.cotf.edu/ete/modules/ msese/explorer.html

Environment and ecology sites
World Wildlife Fund	http://www.wwf.org/
Environment Search Engine	http://www.webdirectory.com/
Greenpeace	http://www.greenpeace.org/
Environment On-line	http://www.solstice.crest.org/ environment/eol/toc.html

Volcano and earthquake sites
Cascade Volcano Observatory	http://vulcan.wr.usgs.gov/
Volcano World	http://volcano.und.nodak.edu/
Global Earthquake Response Center	http://www.earthquake.org/
Savage Earth	http://www.pbs.org/wnet/savageearth/

Weather sites
Met. Office	http://www.met-office.gov.uk
BBC Weather Centre	http://www.bbc.co.uk/weather/
The Weather Channel	http://www.weather.com/twc/ homepage.twc
Hurricane and Storm Tracking	http://hurricane.terrapin.com/
National Weather Service	http://www.nws.noaa.gov/

More amazing and useful sites
World's Tallest Buildings	http://www.worldstallest.com/
The Greatest Places	http://www.greatestplaces.org/
What's It Like Where You Live?	http://www.mobot.org/MBGnet/ sets/index.htm
Mr Dowling's Virtual Classroom	http://www.mrdowling.com/
Woods Hole Oceanographic Institute	http://www.whoi.edu
Soil Science Education Page	http://ltpwww.gsfc.nasa.gov/globe/ index.htm
Virtual Cave	http://www.goodearth.com/ virtmap.html
Glaciers	http://www.glacier.rice.edu/
United Nations Homepage	http://www.un.org/

INDEX

In this index, page numbers in *italic* show where to find pictures. Words that have a lot of page numbers usually have a number in **bold** to show where to find the main explanation.